horses&ponies

horses & ponies

Senior Editors Shaila Brown, Steven Carton
Project Editor Amanda Wyatt
Editorial Assistant Zaina Budaly
US Editor Heather Wilcox
Senior Art Editor Jacqui Swan
Designers Joe Lawrence, Anna Pond, Mary Sandberg, Louise Dick
Illustrators Clarisse Hassan, Simon/KJA Artists, Arran Lewis
Picture Researchers Sarah Hopper, Geetika Bhandari, Rituraj Singh
Managing Editors Rachel Fox, Lisa Gillespie
US Executive Editor Lori Hand
Managing Art Editor Owen Peyton Jones
Production Editor Gillian Reid
Production Controller Meskerem Berhane
Jacket Designer Surabhi Wadhwa
Publisher Andrew Macintyre
Art Director Karen Self
Publishing Director Jonathan Metcalf
Writer Caroline Stamps
Consultant Margaret Linington-Payne

First American Edition, 2021
Published in the United States by DK Publishing
1450 Broadway, Suite 801, New York, NY 10018

Copyright © 2021 Dorling Kindersley Limited
DK, a Division of Penguin Random House LLC
21 22 23 10 9 8 7 6 5 4 3 2 1
001–319150–Apr/2021

A catalog record for this book
is available from the Library of Congress.
ISBN 978-0-7440-2755-6

DK books are available at special discounts when purchased in bulk for sales promotions, premiums, fund-raising, or educational use. For details, contact: DK Publishing Special Markets, 1450 Broadway, Suite 801, New York, NY 10018
SpecialSales@dk.com

Printed and bound in China

For the curious
www.dk.com

MIX
Paper from
responsible sources
FSC™ C018179
FSC
www.fsc.org

This book was made with Forest Stewardship Council ™ certified paper – one small step in DK's commitment to a sustainable future. For more information go to www.dk.com/our-green-pledge

THE HORSE FAMILY

INSIDE OUT

HORSE BREEDS

The horse family

Early horses

Today's horses evolved from forest-dwelling animals that fed on bushes and trees. They were small and had separate toes on each foot instead of a single hoof. Over time, their legs became longer, allowing them to run faster. Below you can see the important ways their bodies gradually evolved into the horse that we know today.

The skull was longer.

MIDDLE HORSE

Mesohippus, meaning "middle horse," lived about 40 million years ago. It was slightly bigger than *Hyracotherium* and had features it shared with both early horses (such as separate toes) and modern horses (longer limbs and skull). It was a leaf-eater.

EARLY HORSE

Hyracotherium was a forest-living early horse that lived more than 55 million years ago. It was no bigger than a small dog and, had small teeth that were suited to eating leaves and fruit.

The skull was small and narrow.

The back was short and rounded.

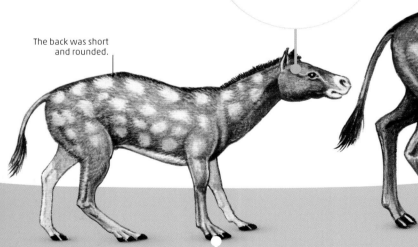

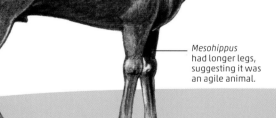

Mesohippus had longer legs, suggesting it was an agile animal.

HEIGHT
14 in (35 cm)

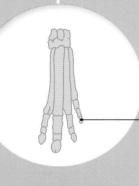

Hyracotherium had four toes on each foot instead of a hoof.

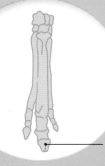

HEIGHT
18 in (45 cm)

Mesohippus had three toes instead of four—most of the weight was placed on its center toe.

The skull was similar to that of a modern horse.

PLAINS GRAZER

Merychippus was one of the first grass-eating horses, appearing about 17 million years ago. It had longer legs than the earlier species, helping it to run fast and even break into a gallop to escape from predators on the open grasslands. *Merychippus* also had a single weight-bearing toe on each foot—it had remnants of other toes, but these didn't reach the ground. The single toe eventually evolved to form a hoof.

The head was broad.

The back was longer and straighter, with more rounded hindquarters.

The neck was longer, making grazing easier.

The legs were slender and long, which increased the horse's stride length.

There is evidence that horses were tamed by the people of central Asia at least **4,000 years ago**.

Over time, the side toes became smaller.

Merychippus was the first one-toed horse.

HEIGHT
48 in (122 cm)

2000 BCE

ANCIENT CHARIOT WITH SPOKED WHEELS

Spoked wheels are just as strong as solid wheels, but are considerably lighter.

With the invention of the spoked wheel, carts became lighter. Evidence of horse bones found alongside chariots suggests that the development of this lighter wheel led to horses being able to pull chariots.

c. 3200 BCE

LJUBLJANA MARSHES WHEEL AND AXLE

The Ljubljana Marshes Wheel, found in Slovenia, is the earliest known wheel, as it dates back about 5,200 years. The first wheels were heavy, solid discs made of wood. The invention of the wheel soon led to simple carts being made, which were often pulled by oxen.

1345 BCE

The Kikkuli text is an early horse-training manual. It was written on four clay tablets in about 1345 BCE by a horse trainer named Kikkuli in the Hittite New Kingdom (in modern-day Turkey). The manual outlines a system designed to get horses to peak fitness, and includes advice on exercise, feeding, and washing them.

KIKKULI TABLET

1300–1200 BCE

The first horse bits were made of rope, bone, leather, or even animal horn. Metal bits began to appear some 3,300 years ago, and were originally made of bronze (a mixture of copper and tin). They are now made of stainless steel.

ANCIENT BRONZE BIT WITH JOINTED MOUTHPIECE

The horse's reins attached to the ring.

1600s

Horses were extinct in North America for thousands of years until the arrival of the Spanish conquistadors, with their Spanish-bred horses. Native Americans were soon using horses for transportation, hunting, and bartering between tribes.

1162–1227

Genghis Khan, the first leader of the vast Mongol Empire, used horses to capture huge areas of land. His armies were skilled at fighting on horseback, and horses also provided the armies with food and clothing.

c. 1760–1840

During the Industrial Revolution in Europe and North America, horses were needed to power new types of machinery, for farming, for working in mines, and for transporting heavy goods.

1860

A fast postal service started in the US, going from Missouri to California. It was known as the Pony Express, and it depended on teams of horses to cover huge distances.

PONY EXPRESS ADVERTISEMENT

Horses and humans

Horses have played a huge role in the lives of humans for thousands of years. Nobody knows exactly when the first person climbed on a horse's back, but we do know about many other key historical events in the relationship between horses and humans. Here are a few of those events.

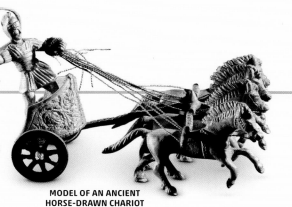

680 BCE

Chariot racing involving two horses or four horses per chariot was introduced to the ancient Olympic Games. The races featured dangerous turns that often caused the chariots to crash or tip over.

MODEL OF AN ANCIENT HORSE-DRAWN CHARIOT AND CHARIOTEER

600 BCE

Polo players use long mallets to hit a wooden ball. This popular game was first played in Persia (modern-day Iran) in around 600 BCE. At that time, it was seen as a good training exercise for mounted soldiers.

The first metal horseshoes were tied on, and not nailed on as they are now.

910 CE

The first written record of a metal horseshoe dates to about this time. Horses did wear shoes before then, but they were made of plant material and animal hide.

EARLY IRON HORSESHOE

c. 343 BCE

Bucephalus, a mighty stallion, belonged to Alexander the Great, an ancient Greek king. It is said that Alexander tamed him as a boy when no one else could. Bucephalus was used as a battle horse, and after the horse died, Alexander named a city after him.

Alexander and Bucephalus appear in this ancient Roman floor mosaic.

1912

The Olympic Games in Stockholm, Sweden, saw the introduction of new equestrian sports: dressage, show jumping, and eventing.

Today

Horses are now are a part of various sports, but they're also ridden just for fun. Although horses aren't widely used in factories anymore, the term "horsepower" is still used as a measurement of an engine's power.

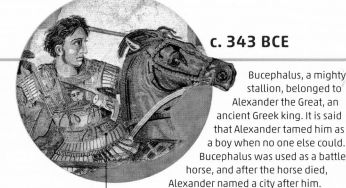

Long **before horses were tamed**, people painted images of them onto cave walls.

In 1969, two archaeologists discovered a cave in a mountainous region of northern Spain, now known as the Ekain Cave. Inside, they found wall paintings that date back to about 14,000 years ago, many of which are of horses. The paintings reveal how, at that time, horses weren't ridden but instead hunted by the early humans.

Who's who?

The domestic horse is part of a small family of closely related species of horses, asses, and zebras. Together, they are known as equids. Each member of the family has special traits that make them suited to different environments and activities.

KIANG

The Kiang is a wild ass that lives on the grasslands of the Tibetan plateau in China and parts of northern India. It is the largest of the wild asses. Kiangs have a dark, broad stripe that runs from the mane along the back and down the wispy tail.

ASIAN WILD ASS

This donkeylike equid is also known as the onager. It is similar to the African wild ass (below right), but larger. Surprisingly, given their short legs, they can reach and even exceed the speed of a racehorse.

ZEBRA

For protection, plains zebras live in big herds on vast areas of grass in Africa known as savannas. They are the most common of all zebras—there are two other types: Grevy's and Mountain. No two zebras have the same pattern of stripes.

DOMESTIC HORSE

The horse we recognize today is a result of hundreds of years of specialized breeding. In spite of this, they still have the instincts learned from millions of years as a prey animal and are constantly alert to danger.

Plains zebras have distinct black and white stripes.

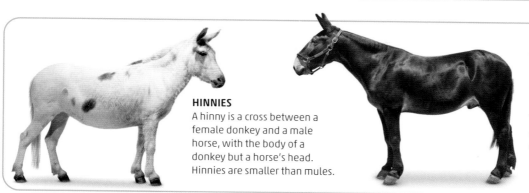

HINNIES

A hinny is a cross between a female donkey and a male horse, with the body of a donkey but a horse's head. Hinnies are smaller than mules.

MULES

A mule is a cross between a male donkey and a female horse. Mules have heads that look like that of a donkey but bodies that look like a horse. They are incredibly strong and are used around the world for all sorts of work.

Although horses, asses, and zebras **look different**, they can all **breed together** to produce young.

PRZEWALSKI'S HORSE

This horse was once thought to be the only true wild horse, but many experts now consider it to be a descendant of the domestic horse. They live in the wild, but had to be reintroduced from captive-bred horses after the last of the Przewalski's horses in the wild died.

AFRICAN WILD ASS

This equid is notable for the stripes on its legs known as leg bars, which are always black. It also has a narrow, faint stripe that runs the length of its back. They are hardy animals and can survive in deserts with little water.

DOMESTIC DONKEY

The donkey is a subspecies of the African wild ass—both have long ears and long muzzles. Donkeys have been used by people for at least 5,000 years.

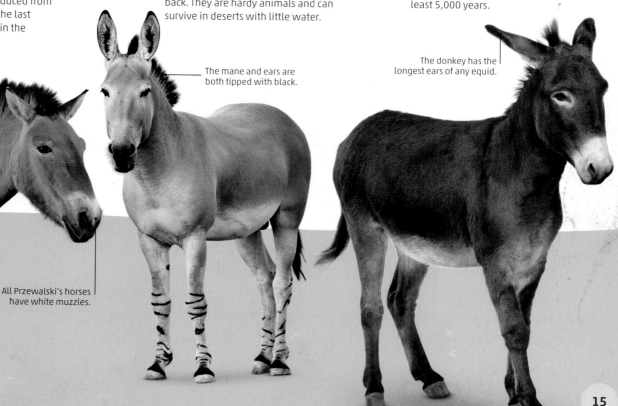

The mane and ears are both tipped with black.

The donkey has the longest ears of any equid.

All Przewalski's horses have white muzzles.

ALBERTA MOUNTAIN HORSES

Nicknamed "Wildies," these horses wander the eastern slopes of the Rocky Mountains in Alberta, Canada. There are hundreds of Alberta Mountain Horses today. They live in small herds for protection and companionship.

BANKER HORSES

These horses are found on the tiny islands off the east coast of North Carolina. Living on an island can be tough, but the Banker Horses have found clever ways to survive. Some have even learned to dig a hole in the sand to find fresh water. They also sometimes swim between islands to find better grazing. Banker Horses are thought be descended from domesticated Spanish horses brought to the Americas in the 16th century.

In the wild

There are no longer any truly wild horse or pony breeds in the world, as all of them have been tamed and used by people for various tasks at some point in history. However, there are thousands of horses that still live in a semi-wild state with little or no control from people. Descended from domesticated breeds that have escaped or been released, they gather in herds and are known as "feral" or "semi-feral." Many of the feral herds are free to roam over vast areas of land.

NEW FOREST PONIES

There have been ponies living in the New Forest in southern England since the 11th century. Today, ponies still graze freely in the New Forest, but they all have owners who pay an annual fee for their right to graze on this common land. Herds owned by the same person have their tails cut into a particular pattern—the tail cut shows that fees have been paid.

MISAKI

The Misaki horses may have descended from horses brought to Japan from central Asia in the 6th century. They were first written about in 1697, when a small herd was rounded up so that it could be used to breed more horses for farm work. The Misaki lives on Kyūshū, Japan's third-largest island, and is now one of the world's rarest breeds. There are thought to be only about a hundred left, and those that remain are protected by the Japanese government.

NAMIB DESERT HORSES

The Namib Desert in southern Africa is a harsh place to live, and yet small herds of horses have managed to scratch out a living since being released there in the early 1900s. In recent decades, local companies have provided supplies of extra food for these tough horses, as well as access to clean water.

BRUMBIES

A brumby is a feral horse that roams free in the Australian bush. Brumbies exist in many thousands, and a group is known as a "mob" or a "band." Like most feral horses, brumbies are descendants of horses that escaped or were released by their owners who no longer needed them. They face a lot of hardships, including water shortages and bushfires, but have proved to be great survivors.

In the wild, **herds of horses roam the landscape** in much the same way as their ancestors did thousands of years ago.

Przewalski's horses live on the grassy steppes of Central Asia, and often wander in groups of several mares, a dominant stallion, and their offspring. These horses have the ability to thrive in a hostile climate. They are wild and spirited by nature and, much like the zebra, they have never been domesticated.

Inside out

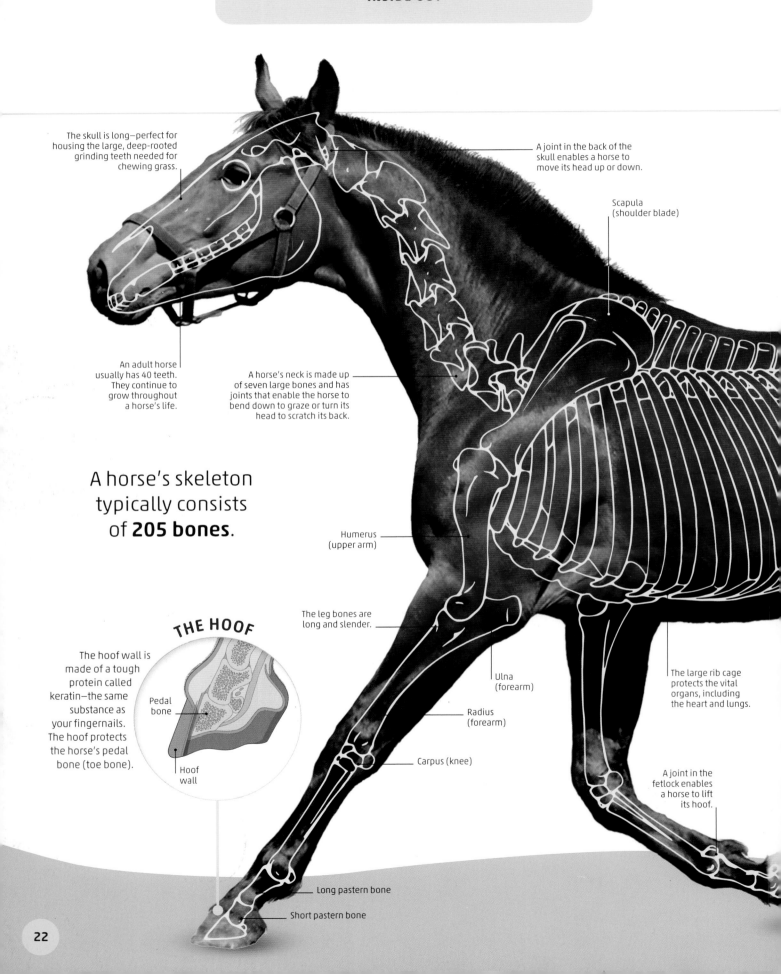

The skull is long—perfect for housing the large, deep-rooted grinding teeth needed for chewing grass.

A joint in the back of the skull enables a horse to move its head up or down.

Scapula (shoulder blade)

An adult horse usually has 40 teeth. They continue to grow throughout a horse's life.

A horse's neck is made up of seven large bones and has joints that enable the horse to bend down to graze or turn its head to scratch its back.

A horse's skeleton typically consists of **205 bones**.

Humerus (upper arm)

THE HOOF

The hoof wall is made of a tough protein called keratin—the same substance as your fingernails. The hoof protects the horse's pedal bone (toe bone).

Pedal bone

Hoof wall

The leg bones are long and slender.

Ulna (forearm)

The large rib cage protects the vital organs, including the heart and lungs.

Radius (forearm)

Carpus (knee)

A joint in the fetlock enables a horse to lift its hoof.

Long pastern bone

Short pastern bone

Built to run

STURDY SPINE

A horse's vertebral column (spine) is made up of 29 bones—Arab horses, however, have one less. The spine is strong and rigid, enabling a horse to carry tremendous weight.

A horse is built for speed—its main form of defense against predators. Its skeleton is strong, but flexible enough to allow it to stretch out into a gallop or bend to graze.

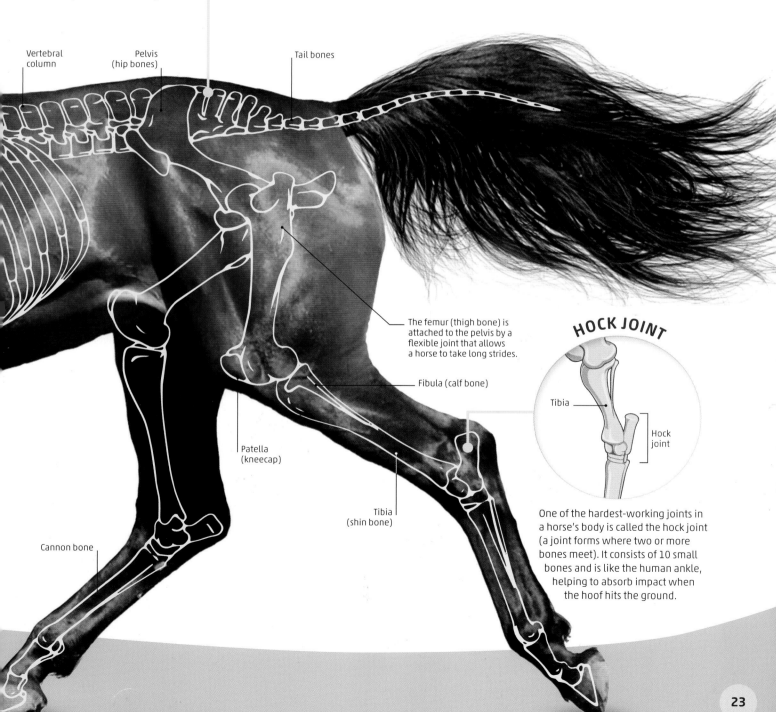

Vertebral column

Pelvis (hip bones)

Tail bones

The femur (thigh bone) is attached to the pelvis by a flexible joint that allows a horse to take long strides.

Fibula (calf bone)

HOCK JOINT

Tibia

Hock joint

Patella (kneecap)

Tibia (shin bone)

Cannon bone

One of the hardest-working joints in a horse's body is called the hock joint (a joint forms where two or more bones meet). It consists of 10 small bones and is like the human ankle, helping to absorb impact when the hoof hits the ground.

Body shapes

A horse's body shape is known as its "conformation." An ideal body shape, or "good conformation," has good bone structure, with all body parts in proportion and symmetrical limbs. Having good conformation for its breed, like this Morgan, makes a horse more likely to stay injury-free.

THE POINTS OF A HORSE

Do you know what a poll is? Or a dock? Or a hock? These are all different body parts—known as the points—of a horse. Riding instructors will often refer to your horse's various points during a lesson, so it's helpful to learn their names.

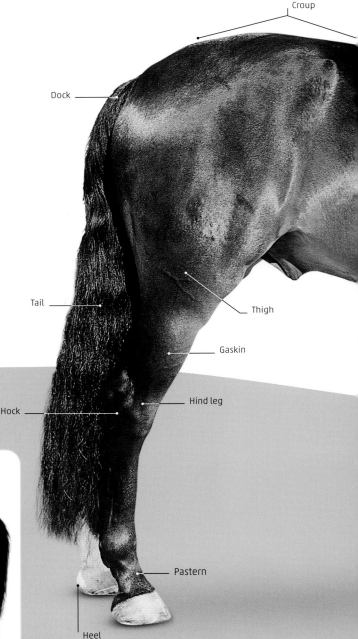

Croup

Dock

Tail

Thigh

Gaskin

Hock

Hind leg

Pastern

Heel

DIFFERENT BODY SHAPES

Horses are bred for different activities, from carrying heavy loads to racing, so the ideal conformation differs depending on the type of horse. A horse can have good conformation for one activity but poor conformation for another.

BRETON

Breton horses have been bred to have strong, muscular bodies, which are suitable for hauling heavy loads on farms.

CRIOLLO

A criollo is a South American horse with lots of stamina. It's able to travel large distances across rocky ground thanks to its small, tough hooves.

MEASURING HEIGHT

A horse's height is measured in hands high (hh), from the ground to the top of the withers. Long ago, people measured horses using their hands, until the measurement was set at 4 in (10 cm). Today, measuring sticks are used and measurements can be given in meters and centimeters, as well as hands high.

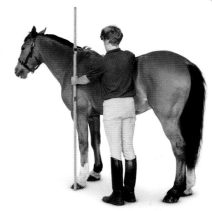

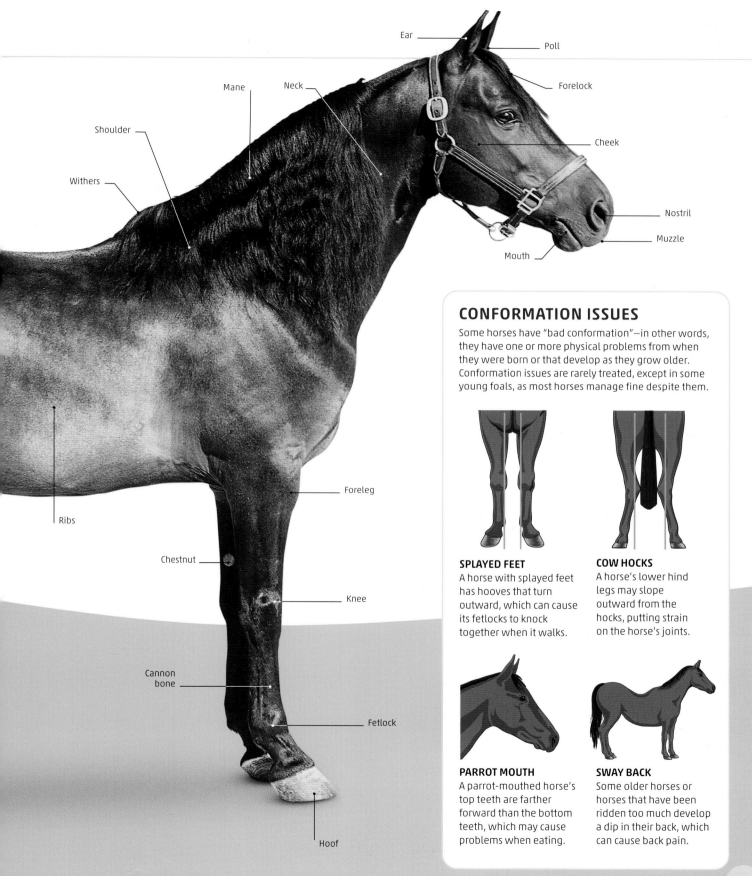

Ear
Poll
Forelock
Mane
Neck
Shoulder
Cheek
Withers
Nostril
Muzzle
Mouth
Foreleg
Ribs
Chestnut
Knee
Cannon bone
Fetlock
Hoof

CONFORMATION ISSUES

Some horses have "bad conformation"—in other words, they have one or more physical problems from when they were born or that develop as they grow older. Conformation issues are rarely treated, except in some young foals, as most horses manage fine despite them.

SPLAYED FEET
A horse with splayed feet has hooves that turn outward, which can cause its fetlocks to knock together when it walks.

COW HOCKS
A horse's lower hind legs may slope outward from the hocks, putting strain on the horse's joints.

PARROT MOUTH
A parrot-mouthed horse's top teeth are farther forward than the bottom teeth, which may cause problems when eating.

SWAY BACK
Some older horses or horses that have been ridden too much develop a dip in their back, which can cause back pain.

Horses in a herd take turns to **nap standing up** while others stay on lookout duty.

Unlike humans, horses can sleep standing up. They doze for short periods several times a day, with their legs locked into position. This allows them to relax without tumbling over. However, they still lie down to have a deep sleep for a few hours at night.

Senses

Horses have the same five senses as humans—sight, hearing, smell, touch, and taste—but theirs are much sharper than ours. As grazing prey animals, horses are on high alert for signs of danger. They constantly absorb information about their surroundings through their senses, ready to react in an instant to the sight or smell of a predator. Horses are also incredibly good at reading human faces—if you look nervous they'll be scared too, so try to be calm in their presence.

AREAS OF VISION

A horse's two eyes work independently of each other. Each eye has a separate area of vision the shape of a semicircle. Behind and immediately in front of the horse are blind spots, which is why you must always approach from the side.

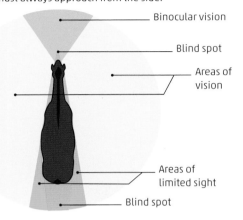

- Binocular vision
- Blind spot
- Areas of vision
- Areas of limited sight
- Blind spot

PESKY FLIES

A horse's highly developed sense of touch means it can feel a tiny fly landing on its body and flick its tail at the precise spot to remove it. This highly developed sensitivity might mean a horse startles if it is touched unexpectedly.

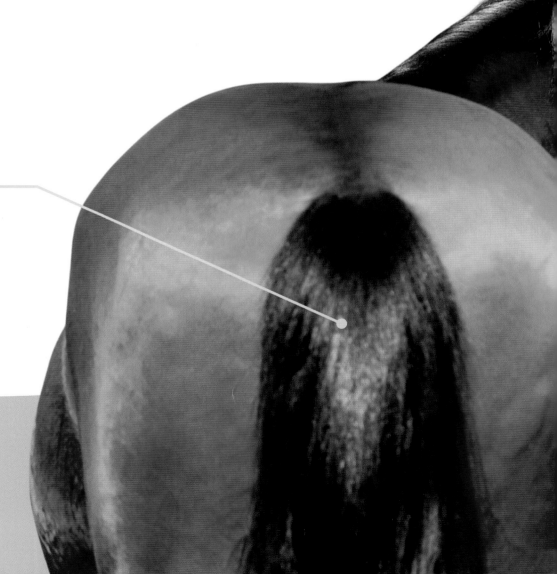

POWERFUL SIGHT

Horses have the largest eyes of any mammal on land and much better vision than humans, particularly at night. They can't detect as many colors as humans, however. They can see yellow, green, and blue well but it's much harder for them to see red and orange.

PRECISE HEARING

Without moving their heads, horses can pick up sounds that come from different directions by moving each of their ears independently. Their large ears act as funnels, constantly capturing sounds that most humans wouldn't be able to hear.

KEEN SENSE OF SMELL

Horses use their sense of smell to check their food or recognize familiar horses or humans. If a horse detects a new or unusual smell, it may curl up its top lip and inhale air over the sensitive membrane underneath—an action known as "flehmen." Mares and their newborn foals do this to learn each others' scents.

SENSITIVE TOUCH

Like many mammals, horses have whiskers—long hairs growing from their faces that are sensitive to the slightest touch. As horses can't see directly in front of their noses, whiskers help them to sense nearby objects.

ON HIGH ALERT

If a horse sees or hears something that might be a threat, it will only turn its head, not its body, in that direction, to identify the danger—it can run away faster that way.

How horses move

Both wild and stabled horses have four natural ways of moving, called "gaits." Most horses walk, trot, canter, and gallop, but some breeds are taught other specialized gaits known as "ambling gaits."

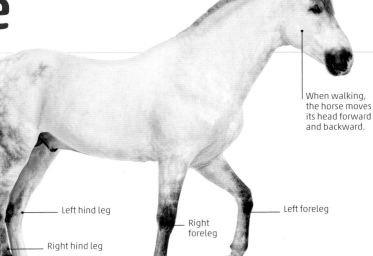

When walking, the horse moves its head forward and backward.

Left hind leg

Right hind leg

Right foreleg

Left foreleg

NATURAL GAITS

Whether a horse is walking, trotting, cantering, or galloping is determined by the pattern in which its legs move and the rhythm that's created when its feet touch the ground. Each of the natural gaits has a rhythm of two, three, or four beats—the number of times one or more of the horse's feet land on the ground before the pattern restarts.

WALK

A walk is the slowest movement. It's a four-beat gait in which two or three feet are always on the ground. The legs move in a pattern: the left hind leg touches down first, then the left fore, followed by the right hind, and then the right fore. Horses usually walk at about 4 mph (6 km/h).

The left hind leg on the ground propels the horse forward.

The right hind leg will lower and touch the ground at the same time as the left foreleg.

Right foreleg

Left foreleg

CANTER

A canter is a smooth, three-beat gait, usually between 10 and 17 mph (16 and 27 km/h). One of the horse's hind legs (here, the left hind) propels the horse forward, while the other three are off the ground. This horse's right hind and left forelegs will then come down together, followed by the right foreleg.

AMBLING GAITS

Some horses can be taught to move in different ways than their natural gaits. These specialized "ambling gaits" are faster than a walk but usually slower than a canter.

PACE

For a pace, the horse moves its legs on each side together, right side, then left side, resulting in a fast walk. A pace gait is often used in two-wheeled harness races.

TÖLT

Icelandic horses have a fast-paced, four-beat walk known as a tölt, in which the forelegs are brought up high. It's a comfortable pace for the rider over long distances.

RUNNING WALK

Tennessee Walking Horses can perform a smooth but fast running walk. It's almost a mix of walk and trot, where the front legs trot while the back legs take walking strides.

A horse trots at about 8 mph (13 km/h).

The right foreleg is paired with the left hind leg.

The left hind leg moves forward at the same time as the right foreleg.

TROT

A trotting horse uses its legs in diagonal pairs, moving the right foreleg and left hind forward together, followed by the left foreleg and the right hind. The trot is a two-beat gait. When riding a trotting horse, it's more comfortable to rise out of the saddle on every other beat, an action known as "posting."

GALLOP

A gallop is a horse's top speed—it can be as fast as 25-30 mph (40-48 km/h). It's a four-beat movement and at one point all four hooves are in the air. Most horses can only gallop 2 miles (3 km) before resting as it requires a lot of energy.

When all four hooves are off the ground, the legs are bent.

FREEDOM!

Release a horse into a paddock and it will often raise its tail, hold its head high, and trot about looking very pleased with itself. It's expressing pleasure and excitement.

ANGRY EARS

The position of a horse's ears can tell us a lot about what the horse is thinking. If the ears are laid flat back against the head, for example, it can mean the horse is angry.

FEELING SCARED?

Some horses have eyes with a white area that is visible all the time, but if a horse with solid-colored eyes suddenly widens them and flashes their white areas, it may signal fear.

Mutual grooming helps both horses to scratch all the places that are hard to reach, such as their hindquarters.

This horse is using its teeth to gently scratch its friend.

YOU'RE TOO CLOSE!

One way a horse will show its displeasure is by kicking out its hind legs. It may be protecting a foal, as shown here, or simply warning another horse to keep its distance.

MOVE NOW!

A stallion rounds up its mares by pinning its ears back, stretching its neck, and keeping its head low. This movement is called "snaking" as the horse's head resembles that of a snake.

STRESSED OUT

If horses get bored, stressed out, or sad, they may develop bad habits, such as crib biting in which they bite a gate, fence, or post and pull back on it while sucking in air.

How horses talk

You may think horses can't talk, but actually they're communicating all the time. With the twitch of an ear, a swish of the tail, and a turn of the head, a horse can tell the rest of its herd how it feels or if something's happening. Horses use their body language (the movements of their bodies) to communicate with each other. Watch closely and you might be able to understand what they're thinking.

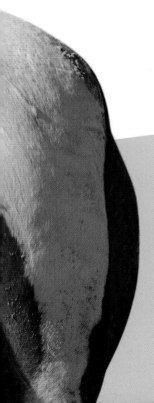

SOUND DECODER

Horses make all sorts of noises. Most people know that they neigh, but they also snort and nicker. Knowing what each sound means can help you guess how a horse is feeling.

NEIGH
A neighing sound is a horse saying to another horse, "Hello! Look at me."

SNORT
A snort is a sharp release of breath, made by a horse when it's excited or unsure about something.

NICKER
A nicker is a low, rumbling sound made by a happy horse. Horses may nicker when they recognize their friends.

MUTUAL GROOMING

Just like people make friendships, horses form close bonds with other horses. If a horse is particularly friendly with another (they do have best friends!), they will regularly groom each other by nibbling at each other's backs. It's an activity that all horses appear to enjoy.

A stallion **rears up and fights** to defend its position.

This pair of mustangs is fighting, as one stallion has challenged the other for the right to take over the herd. Fights such as this are usually very short, with the loser making a quick retreat, and the winner gaining in status.

Colors and markings

From bay to gray, horses come in a wide range of colors. Many also have distinct markings on their faces and legs. All of these different colors and markings have specific names to describe them.

COAT COLORS

Some breeds are bred to be specific colors—for example, a Lippizaner horse is usually gray, while Appaloosa horses always have spotted coats. Other breeds come in a range of colors: a Shetland pony can be any color, except spotted.

BAY
The most common color, bay horses are reddish brown with black manes, tails, and lower legs.

CHESTNUT
Chestnut coats range from pale to dark reddish brown, with a similar-colored mane and tail.

BROWN
Brown horses have a mixture of black and brown hairs. They have brown manes, tails, and legs.

PALOMINO
This color horse is yellow or golden with a white or cream mane and tail.

DUN
As well as partly black legs, sandy yellow duns have a black tail, mane, and stripe on their back.

STRAWBERRY ROAN
Strawberry roans have chestnut hair mixed with white hair. Roans may also be blue or red.

GRAY
A gray coat has a mixture of black and white hairs on black skin. The shade can vary from light to dark.

BLACK
Black horses are unusual to see. Some black horses may have white markings.

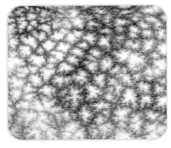

DAPPLE GRAY
This coat has dark gray rings (dapples) on a light gray base, or light gray rings on a dark gray base.

PIEBALD
A piebald coat has black and white patches. A coat with brown and white patches is called "skewbald."

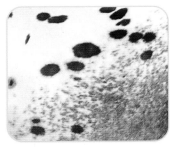

SPOTTED
Also called Appaloosa, horses with coats covered in small spots have spotted skin.

FACE MARKINGS

Some horses have white markings on their faces, which can help to identify individuals in a herd. Face markings can be lots of different shapes but some are more commonly seen than others.

WHITE FACE
In contrast to its coat, a horse may have a totally white face. Some white-faced horses are blue-eyed.

STAR
A small white marking centered between or above a horse's eyes is known as a star.

SNIP
Some horses have a thin strip of white hair extending from their muzzle a little way up the face.

BLAZE
A blaze is a narrow or wide strip of white hair that runs down the face, between the eyes, to the muzzle.

LEG MARKINGS

Black, brown, or chestnut colored horses sometimes have areas of white hair on one or more of their legs. Some horses have markings that cover only the area immediately above their hooves, while others have markings that extend beyond their knees (on the front leg) or hocks (on the hind leg).

CORONET
This type of marking is a small ring of white hair covering the area just above a horse's hoof.

SOCK
A sock marking ends just above the fetlock, but it doesn't reach as far as a horse's knee or hock.

STOCKING
A stocking extends much farther up a horse's leg, at least as far as its knee or hock.

ERMINE MARKS
Some horses have dark spots that appear on their white markings, just above the hoof.

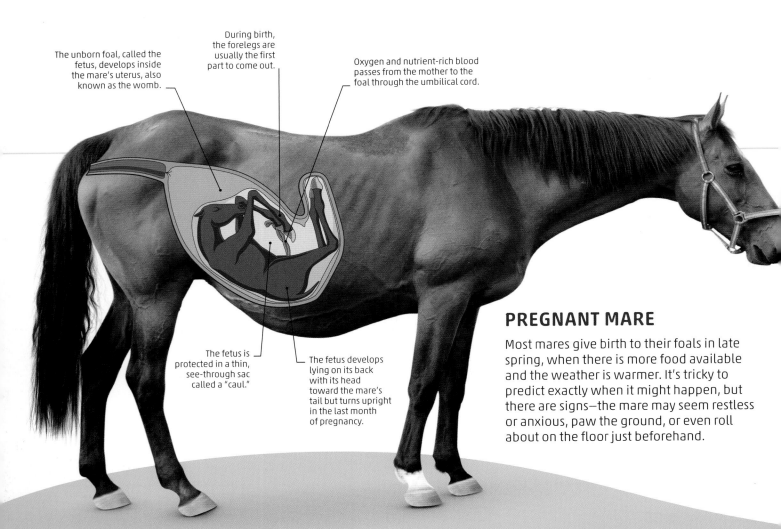

The unborn foal, called the fetus, develops inside the mare's uterus, also known as the womb.

During birth, the forelegs are usually the first part to come out.

Oxygen and nutrient-rich blood passes from the mother to the foal through the umbilical cord.

The fetus is protected in a thin, see-through sac called a "caul."

The fetus develops lying on its back with its head toward the mare's tail but turns upright in the last month of pregnancy.

PREGNANT MARE

Most mares give birth to their foals in late spring, when there is more food available and the weather is warmer. It's tricky to predict exactly when it might happen, but there are signs—the mare may seem restless or anxious, paw the ground, or even roll about on the floor just beforehand.

NEWLY BORN

A mare will usually give birth at night, when it's quiet and she feels safest. It tends to be a speedy process, sometimes only taking an hour. After birth, the mare and foal soon learn to recognize each other, largely through smell.

UP AND READY

A newborn foal will try to stand very quickly after birth by spreading its legs widely apart. It's tricky because its legs are almost as long as its mother's, making them hard to control! But the foal will soon be able to walk and run.

SUCKLING MILK

For the first few months of its life a foal depends on milk, which it suckles (drinks) from the mare's teats, between her hind legs. The first feed is the most important as it contains antibodies—proteins that help to protect the foal from illness.

Mares and foals

HERD RELATIONSHIPS

Ideally a young foal will be brought up in a field with other foals and adult horses, so that it can play and learn. A foal will quickly discover its place in the herd, and be told off with a quick nip from its mother or another older horse if it does something wrong.

A mare, an adult female horse, is usually pregnant for about 11 months before giving birth to its foal. They may look a bit wobbly, but newborn foals have evolved to be on the move quickly so that they can run away from dangerous predators and keep up with their mother. They can usually stand within half an hour of being born, and their eyesight and sense of smell are already highly developed. A foal will stay close by its mother's side for the first few weeks of its life.

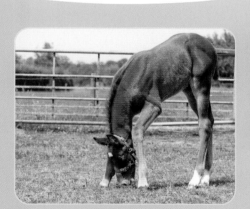

EATING GRASS

A foal starts to nibble grass about 10 days after its birth, copying the way its mother feeds. It's a bit awkward at first, because the foal's legs are so long. By two months old, it drinks less of its mother's milk and grazes more often on grass.

RUNNING AROUND

Foals, like all young animals, have huge amounts of energy and will spend lots of time rushing around exploring their surroundings and playing with other young horses. But all this exercise can tire them out.

SLEEPING

Foals under three months of age spend about 12 hours a day asleep. They sleep in short bursts, having lots of little naps throughout the day. They usually lie down to sleep (unlike adult horses, which largely sleep standing up).

Horse breeds

Types of horse

Scientists don't know the exact origins of the domestic horse but, over time, people realized that different types of horse could be deliberately bred to perform particular tasks. Today, there are more than 350 breeds of horse in the world and they are divided into three main categories: heavy horses, light horses, and ponies.

HEAVY HORSES

Heavy, or draft, horses, such as this Shire horse, are tall, stocky, and muscular. Fully grown, they stand at more than 16.2 hands—that's taller than the average adult man. They move more slowly than light horses but are incredibly strong. In the past, they were used for farm work or hauling huge loads—the term "draft" means dragging or pulling a heavy load.

The muscular hindquarters provide the strength needed to haul heavy loads.

A Shire horse is big—it weighs about the same as 28 10-year-old children.

Heavy horses have stocky, muscular legs.

Many heavy horses have silky long hair on their lower legs.

Each hoof is almost double the length and width of a light horse's hoof.

Light horses have strong, slender legs, ideal for jumping or racing.

GENERAL NAMES

Some horses are known by a general name rather than by a breed name. They are the result of a mixing of breeds and have the same set of characteristics such as speed, stamina, or color. For example, the polo pony is used for a game played on horseback called polo. Polo ponies are bred for their agility and speed, as they have to move quickly across a pitch, twisting and turning to change direction very suddenly.

LIGHT HORSES

These horses are usually above 14.2 hands. Unlike heavy horses, they have narrow bodies and long, slender limbs. They are also more agile and athletic and so make excellent sporting horses—most of the racehorses you see today belong in this category. All light horses can trace their origins to the Arab horse.

A Sardinian Anglo-Arab horse is no more than half the weight of a Shire.

PONIES

Ponies are 14.2 hands or smaller—their legs are shorter than those of a light horse. Ponies tend to be strong and surefooted—many of the breeds can easily carry an adult. They grow thick winter coats that allow them to live outside during the cold months.

A Welsh pony is half the weight of the Sardinian Anglo-Arab horse.

A pony's legs tend to be the same length as the depth of the body.

Light horses

World's oldest breed
ARAB

ORIGIN
Arabian Peninsula

HEIGHT
14.3 hands (150 cm)

COLOR
Bay, gray, chestnut,
or black

The Arab horse is at least 4,500 years old and originated in the Middle East, somewhere between Arabia and Turkey. The earliest known breeders were the Bedouin desert-dwelling people, who valued these horses for their intelligence and beauty.

The Bedouin people used Arab horses as war horses and for transportation. They took great care of their horses, sheltering them from the heat of the desert sun by bringing them into their tents. Today, Arab horses are bred all over the world and play an important role in improving other breeds. Because of their amazing strength and stamina, they are perfect for sports, such as long-distance riding. Arab horses are known for being fiery and courageous—in the 19th century, the French emperor Napoleon Bonaparte chose an Arab stallion named Marengo to ride into many battles. Arab horses have slightly shorter bodies when compared to other horses. They have 17 pairs of ribs, while other horse breeds have 18.

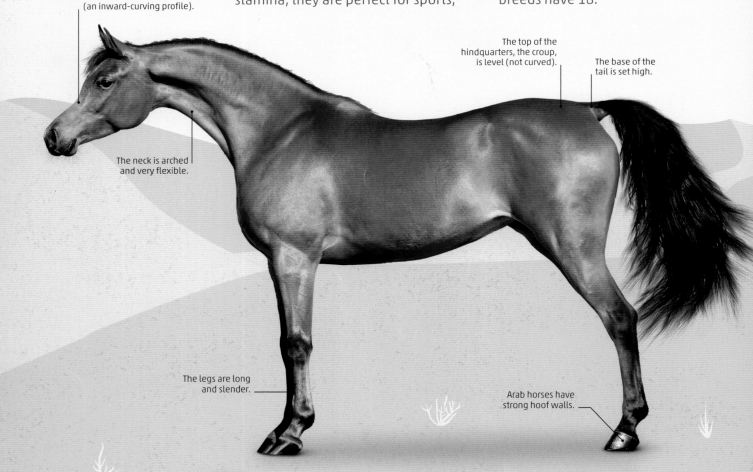

The Arab horse has a distinctive "dished face" (an inward-curving profile).

The top of the hindquarters, the croup, is level (not curved).

The base of the tail is set high.

The neck is arched and very flexible.

The legs are long and slender.

Arab horses have strong hoof walls.

The mane is soft and silky.

The Arab horse's muzzle is small with distinctive flared nostrils.

The Arab is one of the **oldest and most recognizable horse breeds** in the world.

Record-breaker
THOROUGHBRED

ORIGIN
England

HEIGHT
15.2-17 hands
(157-173 cm)

COLOR
Brown, bay, chestnut,
black, or gray

The world's Thoroughbreds can be traced back to three stallions that were brought to England in the late 1600s and early 1700s. Most can be traced to one in particular, the Darley Arabian, a bay brought to England from Syria in 1704.

The breed, the world's fastest over distance, exists thanks to the love of horse racing that rocketed among England's aristocracy in the 1700s. These horses were bred to have the stamina and strength for long races. Today, they are sought after for both flat racing and racing over jumps, with vast sums of money paid for accomplished performers. Like the Arab breed, they are known as "hot-blooded" horses, referring to their spirited, energetic nature.

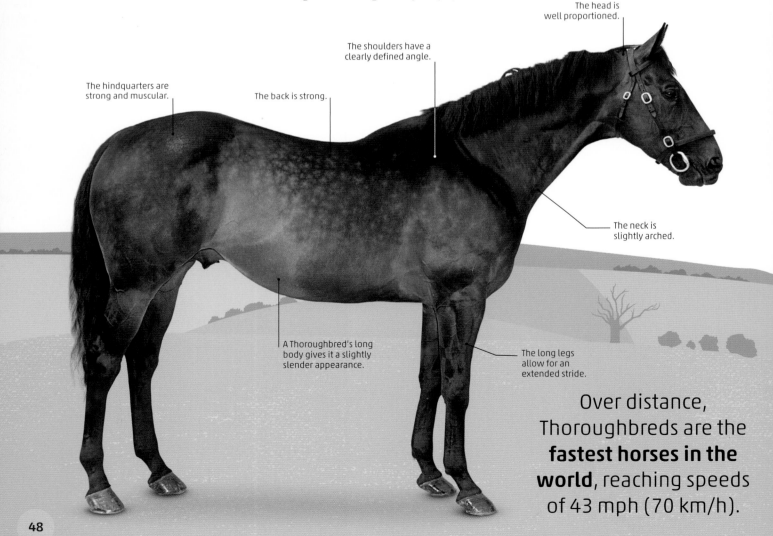

The head is
well proportioned.

The shoulders have a
clearly defined angle.

The hindquarters are
strong and muscular.

The back is strong.

The neck is
slightly arched.

A Thoroughbred's long
body gives it a slightly
slender appearance.

The long legs
allow for an
extended stride.

Over distance,
Thoroughbreds are the
**fastest horses in the
world**, reaching speeds
of 43 mph (70 km/h).

Elegant horse
HACK

ORIGIN
England

HEIGHT
14.2–15.3 hands
(147–160 cm)

COLOR
All solid colors

The hack is not a purebred horse but a type of horse developed for its elegance and suitability for providing a steady ride. It was particularly popular in England in the 1800s, when two types of hack were recognized: the covert hack and the park hack.

Covert hacks were used to carry riders to a hunt, where the rider would then change to another horse (a hunter). Park hacks were bred to be well proportioned, beautiful, and well mannered—they were ridden out in parks by their elegantly dressed owners and were similar to the type of show hack seen today. Hacks are comfortable to ride, and nowadays they are sometimes seen in the show-ring being ridden sidesaddle.

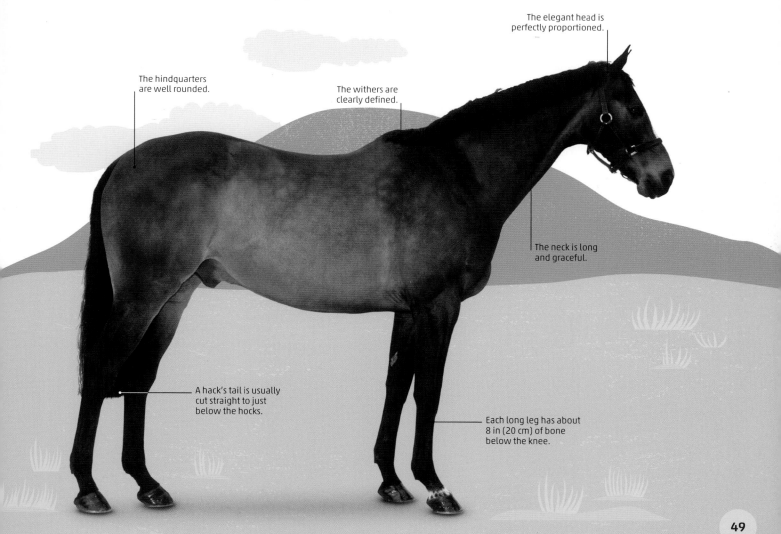

The elegant head is perfectly proportioned.

The hindquarters are well rounded.

The withers are clearly defined.

The neck is long and graceful.

A hack's tail is usually cut straight to just below the hocks.

Each long leg has about 8 in (20 cm) of bone below the knee.

The steeplechase horse is sometimes known as a "**chaser**."

Thoroughbreds are used all over the world for steeplechases—fast-paced races over various jumps and ditches. Jumps can be 4.5 ft (1.3 m) or more in height, and can include water jumps, which require great strength and precision.

Desert horse
BARB

ORIGIN
Morocco

HEIGHT
14.2–15.2 hands
(147–157 cm)

COLOR
Usually gray but also found
in bay, black, or chestnut

The Barb is almost as important as the Arab in terms of the significant influence it has had on European and American breeds. Its origins lie in the desert plains of North Africa, resulting in a hardy, surefooted horse.

In the 8th century, the Barb was used by North African riders. It is supremely adapted to survive high temperatures with little water. It has narrow feet—a trait that helped it move swiftly on the rocky desert landscape from which the breed emerged. The Barb is also known for its stamina and speed, and for being headstrong. Because of these characteristics, the breed has been used to develop important racing breeds, including the Thoroughbred and the American quarter horse.

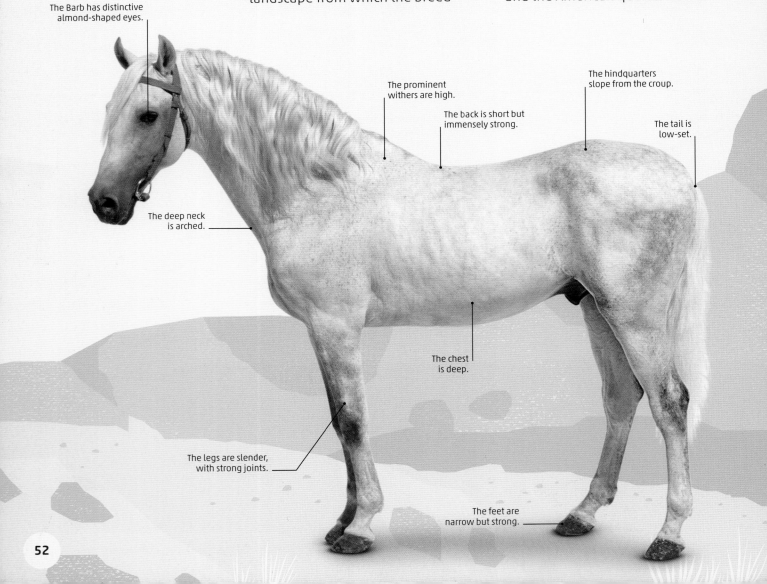

The Barb has distinctive almond-shaped eyes.

The prominent withers are high.

The back is short but immensely strong.

The hindquarters slope from the croup.

The tail is low-set.

The deep neck is arched.

The chest is deep.

The legs are slender, with strong joints.

The feet are narrow but strong.

The tips of the ears are rounded.

The mane is soft and usually left long.

The outline, or profile, of the face is straight or slightly inward curving.

Throughout history, Barb horses have been popular with royalty, including **King Henry VIII of England**, who purchased a number of Barbs in the 16th century.

Hundreds of horses and riders take part in Morocco's Tbourida Grand Prix.

Morocco's Tbourida is a colorful celebration of the country's close bond with its Barb horses. The decorated horses gallop in straight lines, ridden by members of the Berber tribe (also known as the Imazighen) in traditional costume. The spectacle is fast and noisy, with riders often standing up on their stirrups and firing rifles into the air.

This traditional head rope is crafted from horsehair.

The face has a straight profile.

Camargues are known as **"horses of the sea"**— they are just as comfortable in water as they are on land.

Horse of the sea
CAMARGUE

ORIGIN
France

HEIGHT
13–14.2 hands
(132–147 cm)

COLOR
Gray

These semi-wild horses roam freely in the wetlands of the Camargue in the south of France, part of which forms a huge nature reserve. They are branded to identify their owners, but they are only rounded up once a year. They are a protected species.

The freedom to roam the wetlands of the Camargue has made these horses tough and hardy. They survive on what they can find in a largely flooded landscape where plants can be scarce. They breed freely, and when foals are born they are black or brown—their coats turn a striking gray as they mature over a period of four years.

The Camargue is the traditional mount of the Provençal *gardians* (herdsmen), who ride them to round up the black bulls that are bred on local ranches. The *gardians* and Camargues drive the bulls through the region's villages during summer festivals. The calm yet brave nature of these small horses makes them ideal for the task.

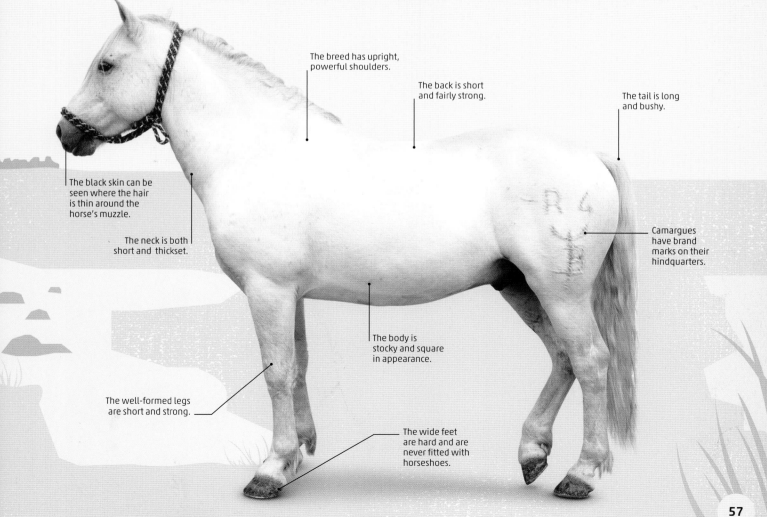

The breed has upright, powerful shoulders.

The back is short and fairly strong.

The tail is long and bushy.

The black skin can be seen where the hair is thin around the horse's muzzle.

The neck is both short and thickset.

Camargues have brand marks on their hindquarters.

The body is stocky and square in appearance.

The well-formed legs are short and strong.

The wide feet are hard and are never fitted with horseshoes.

Pride of Portugal
LUSITANO

ORIGIN
Portugal

HEIGHT
15.1–16.1 hands
(155–165 cm)

COLOR
Gray or any solid color

These agile horses have been selectively bred in Portugal for at least 200 years and are used for riding and for pulling carriages. They have also appeared as dressage horses in the Olympics and regularly take part in major show-jumping events.

Lusitanos are immensely adaptable horses—they are noted for their calm temperament, which makes it possible to train them for a variety of tasks. A famous ceremony takes place once a month at the president's official residence in Lisbon, Portugal, and Lusitanos play a key part. They are used for the changing of the guard, a spectacular ceremony first held in 1910. The ceremony ends with a mounted brass band who carry out some of their performance at a canter. The riders say the Lusitanos have the perfect balance and temperament to be trained for this.

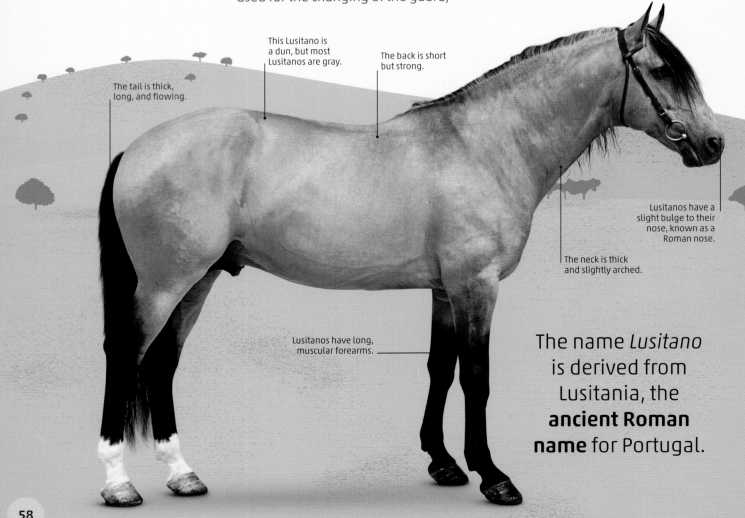

This Lusitano is a dun, but most Lusitanos are gray.

The back is short but strong.

The tail is thick, long, and flowing.

Lusitanos have a slight bulge to their nose, known as a Roman nose.

The neck is thick and slightly arched.

Lusitanos have long, muscular forearms.

The name *Lusitano* is derived from Lusitania, the **ancient Roman name** for Portugal.

58

Champion jumper
SELLE FRANÇAIS

ORIGIN
France

HEIGHT
15.2–17.2 hands
(157–178 cm)

COLOR
Usually chestnut

The Selle Français owes its existence to a breeding program in the early 1800s in northern France, when imported Thoroughbred and half-bred stallions were mixed with local horses. This eventually led to the Selle Français—an outstanding sporting horse.

After World War II (1939–1945), horses in Europe were being used less on farms but were increasingly wanted for riding. The Selle Français, which means "French saddle horse," fitted the demand perfectly. Today, these elegant horses are known for their speed and world-class show-jumping ability—one Selle Français, Baloubet du Rouet, is the only horse to win the show-jumping World Cup three years running. The Selle Français is bold and athletic, but tricky to train.

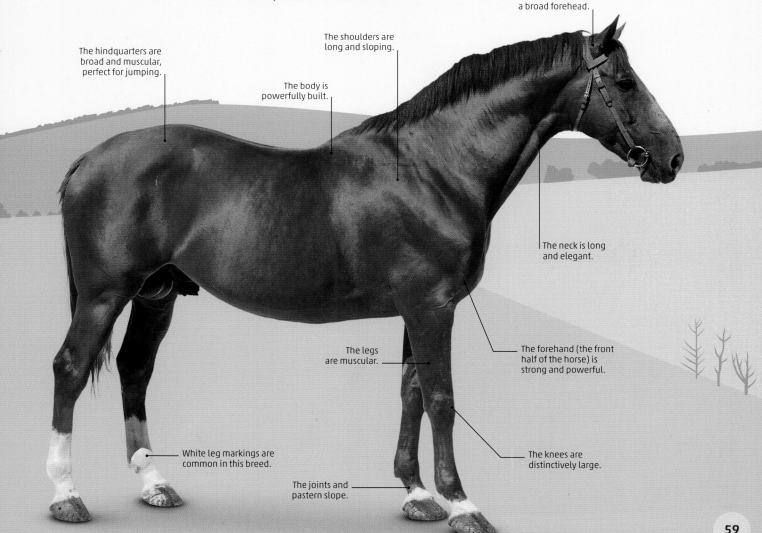

The head is small with a broad forehead.

The shoulders are long and sloping.

The hindquarters are broad and muscular, perfect for jumping.

The body is powerfully built.

The neck is long and elegant.

The legs are muscular.

The forehand (the front half of the horse) is strong and powerful.

White leg markings are common in this breed.

The knees are distinctively large.

The joints and pastern slope.

59

Olympic show jumpers face **leaps of 5.3 ft (1.6 m)** in height.

Selle Français are outstanding show jumpers. Olympic show-jumping events consist of 10–16 obstacles of different heights and widths. Riders race against the clock, and aim to clear all of the obstacles without knocking any over.

Competition horse
HOLSTEINER

ORIGIN
Germany

HEIGHT
16–17 hands
(163–173 cm)

COLOR
Any solid color

There are two types of Holsteiner: classic and modern. The classic is heavy and large-boned. The modern is elegant, lighter, and known for its jumping ability. Its intelligence and even temper make it particularly responsive to training.

The Holsteiner, which dates as far back as 1225, was first bred by monks in northern Germany. It was originally bred as a heavy-bodied agricultural horse. The emergence of the modern Holsteiner can be traced to the late 1800s, when German breeders wanted a handsome coach horse that could double up as a type of riding horse.

Following World War II (1939–1945), German breeders developed the Holsteiner further to create the muscular, world-class show jumper that can be seen today.

The neck is arched and high-set.

The croup slopes slightly.

The withers are defined.

The head of a modern Holsteiner is small, with fine features.

The forearms are muscular.

The hindquarters are muscular.

The cannon bones are both short and strong.

Mountain breed
HAFLINGER

ORIGIN
Austria

HEIGHT
13.3-14.3 hands
(140-150 cm)

COLOR
Chestnut and palomino

The Haflinger is a striking horse, with a chestnut or palomino coat and a flaxen (pale yellow) mane and tail. Bred in mountain areas, Haflingers are noted for their surefootedness and for their good health: they have robust hearts and lungs.

Haflingers were originally used as packhorses and for forestry work in the hillside farms of southern Austria. They can still be seen at work in forested areas of Austria where machines have limited access. Haflingers are also popular riding horses. They are strong enough to carry an adult but are gentle enough to be suitable for a younger rider.

Their heavy look means they are sometimes mistaken for draft horses, but they have no draft horse blood in them. The world's first cloned horse (a horse artificially produced from the cells of another horse) was born to a Haflinger mare in 2003. Named Prometea, she is genetically identical in every way to her mother.

The head is small, with large eyes and small ears.

The flaxen mane and tail are a distinctive feature of the Haflinger.

The back is long and muscular.

The nostrils are wide.

The girth is typically deep.

The hocks are broad and powerful.

The hooves are very hard-wearing.

There is a small amount of hair on the legs.

The cannon bones are short.

Lippizaners mature slowly but **live longer** than most breeds.

The head is straight or slightly convex (outward-curving)

The nostrils are flared.

Dancing horse
LIPPIZANER

ORIGIN
Slovenia

HEIGHT
14.2–15.2 hands
(147–157 cm)

COLOR
Mainly gray
but can also be bay

The development of the Lippizaner can be traced to 1580, when Archduke Charles II of Austria imported 33 Spanish horses. He wanted to breed elegant horses suitable for the nobility. Today's Lippizaners originate from these horses.

Lippizaners are usually born black or bay, but their coat turns white between the ages of six and ten. The occasional adult is bay, and traditionally a bay horse is always kept at the world-famous Spanish Riding School in Vienna, Austria, where they are bred and trained to perform perfectly executed classical dressage. They do not undergo selection for the Spanish Riding School until they are almost four years of age, and the training program then lasts another six years. Lippizaners are calm and intelligent. They are also strong and very willing horses.

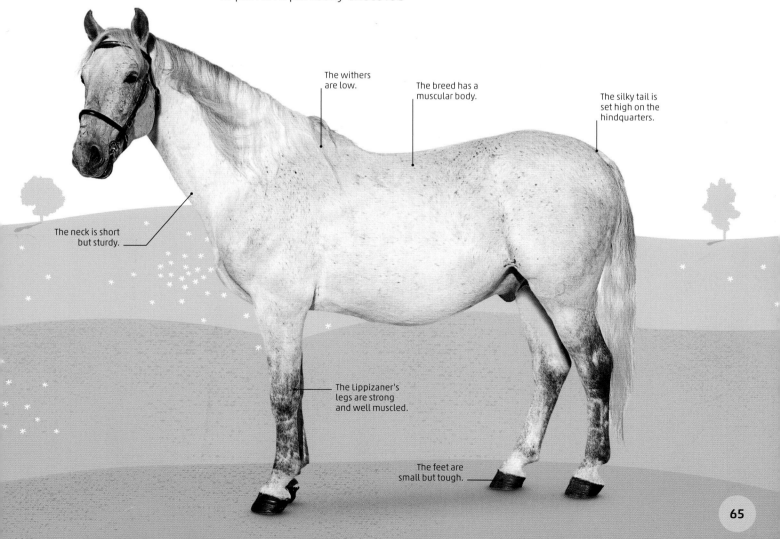

The withers are low.

The breed has a muscular body.

The silky tail is set high on the hindquarters.

The neck is short but sturdy.

The Lippizaner's legs are strong and well muscled.

The feet are small but tough.

Lippizaners can take 10 years to learn the graceful "**airs above the ground**."

The capriole is a movement that sees the Lippizaner leap high into the air, kick out its hind legs, and then land on all four legs at once. It is the most difficult of all the "airs above the ground" that horses perform at the Spanish Riding School in Vienna, Austria.

A horse for royalty
ANDALUCIAN

ORIGIN
Spain

HEIGHT
15–17 hands
(152–172 cm)

COLOR
Usually gray or bay

Noted for its distinctive, high-stepping movement and particularly long stride, the Andalucian is one of the oldest purebred breeds. It is featured in many historical paintings, often shown carrying members of the European nobility.

The influence of the Andalucian can be seen in many other breeds, including the Lippizaner and the Lusitano in Europe and the criollo and quarter horse in America. The Andalucian almost disappeared in the 1830s due to a disease that killed many Spanish horses. The breed owes its survival to a small herd that was kept at a monastery near Seville in Spain. The Andalucian is an athletic, good-looking horse with strong limbs. Riders who train them for dressage say they are quick to learn complicated moves.

The ears are small.

The horse's thick mane is often wavy.

The croup is well rounded.

The back is muscular and almost straight.

The long tail is low-set.

The neck is long, with an elegant arch.

The chest is both wide and round.

The breed's legs are strong and muscular.

The knee is lean and well developed.

The Andalucian has very little hair on the lower legs.

Endangered horse
SALERNO

ORIGIN
Italy

HEIGHT
16 hands (163 cm)

COLOR
Any solid color

The Salerno is an athletic, good-natured horse with a talent for jumping. But, despite such qualities, the Salerno is a rare breed. In 1990, there were thought to be only about 100 Salernos in the world, and in 2007, the breed was listed as endangered.

Salernos were originally known as Persanos—they were developed at the Persano Stud in Italy, which was established in 1763 by King Charles III of Spain. The stud was closed in the 1860s, but the breed survived and was named the Salerno. The stock was improved by crossing it with the Thoroughbred. This produced a larger horse with strong bones, making it an ideal choice for the cavalry—Salernos were used in both World War I (1914–1918) and World War II (1939–1945). Today, Salernos are chosen for leisure riding and for sports, but numbers remain low.

The neck is muscular.

The hair is fine and short.

The hindquarters are powerfully built.

Salernos have fairly wide nostrils.

The legs are strong and slender.

Two of the **greatest Italian show jumpers**, Merano and Posillipo, were Salernos.

The elegant hoof is a characteristic of this breed.

Police horse
KATHIAWARI

ORIGIN
India

HEIGHT
15 hands (152 cm)

COLOR
Any color except black

The most noticeable feature of the Kathiawari is its inward-turning ear tips, which are often able to touch each other. These resilient horses are the choice of India's mounted police, who value their hardiness and willingness to learn.

Kathiawari horses are descended from tough desert war horses. Like all desert horses, they can tolerate heat and are able to survive on little food and water if necessary. They are affectionate, showing great loyalty toward their owners. Kathiawari are used in the sport of tent pegging. This game was originally developed to improve both the horse's and rider's skill in battle against armies that were mounted on elephants. The goal is to gallop toward a small peg and spear it with a lance or sword. It is one of just 10 sports that are recognized by the International Federation for Equestrian Sports.

The short neck tapers up to the head.

The large ears can turn more than 180 degrees.

The shoulders are strong.

The head is held high.

The Kathiawari has a long back.

The thick, bushy tail is low-set.

The muzzle is short.

This Kathiawari is a typical bay, with a reddish-brown body.

The legs are slim but strong.

Of all the horse breeds in the world, the Kathiawari has the **most curved ears**.

Super sprinter
ORLOV TROTTER

ORIGIN
Russia

HEIGHT
16 hands (163 cm)

COLOR
Mostly gray or dapple gray; can also be black or bay

Russia's most famous breed of horse owes its existence to an 18th-century Russian noble, Count Alexei Orlov. The count wanted to breed a horse with a long stride and good endurance for harness racing—in which horses race at a trot, pulling a two-wheeled cart.

Count Orlov owned a huge stud farm in central Russia and had a lot of resources to develop a new breed quickly. It's said that 3,000 horses were involved in the intensive breeding program. The foal that became the breed's foundation stallion was born in 1784. The Orlov Trotter, a particularly elegant horse,

has continued to be improved to this day. Orlovs are traditionally used to pull a Russian *troika*, a carriage or sleigh pulled by three horses that are harnessed side-by-side. The center horse trots, while the horses at each side canter or gallop to keep pace.

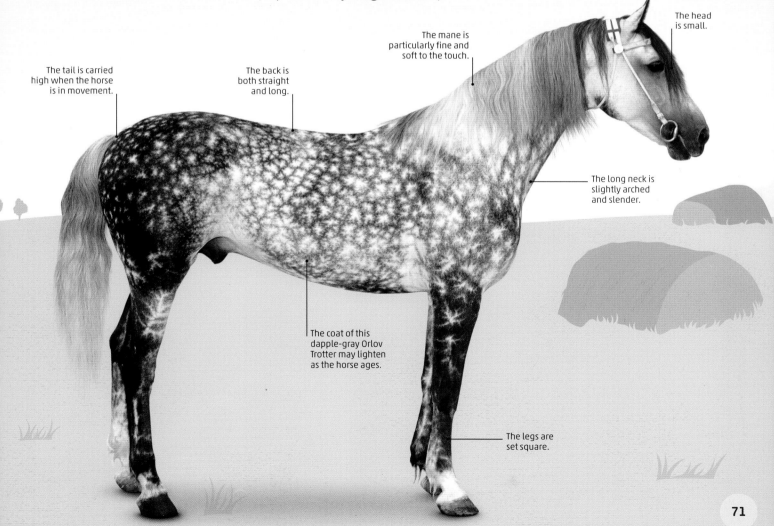

The tail is carried high when the horse is in movement.

The back is both straight and long.

The mane is particularly fine and soft to the touch.

The head is small.

The long neck is slightly arched and slender.

The coat of this dapple-gray Orlov Trotter may lighten as the horse ages.

The legs are set square.

Golden horse
AKHAL-TEKE

ORIGIN
Turkmenistan

HEIGHT
14.3–16 hands
(150–163 cm)

COLOR
Mostly bay, chestnut,
or dun; can also be
black, gray, or silver

The Akhal-Teke gets its nickname of "golden horse" because of its shiny coat, which can sometimes have a metallic glint. The breed has a long history—from humble beginnings to now being highly valued as a racehorse.

The Akhal-Teke is a national emblem of its country of origin, Turkmenistan. Originally a desert breed, it is known for its resilience in conditions of extreme heat. In its homeland, it is valued for its beauty and stamina. In 1935, when Turkmenistan was a part of the Soviet Union, the breed was ordered to be slaughtered by the Soviet government, as it was considered useless—it didn't produce milk or meat. A group of Turkmen people rode Akhal-Tekes to Moscow on a journey of more than 1,550 miles (2,500 km) that took 84 days. A quarter of the trip was across desert, where the horses had little food and water. The aim of the trek was to petition Joseph Stalin, the ruler of the Soviet Union, to save the breed. It worked. The Akhal-Teke is now the Russian sports horse of choice.

The profile is straight.

The withers are high.

The breed has a distinctive narrow and lean-looking body.

The neck is thin and long.

The thighs are long and very muscular.

The coat has a beautiful metallic sheen.

The forelegs are straight and can be close together.

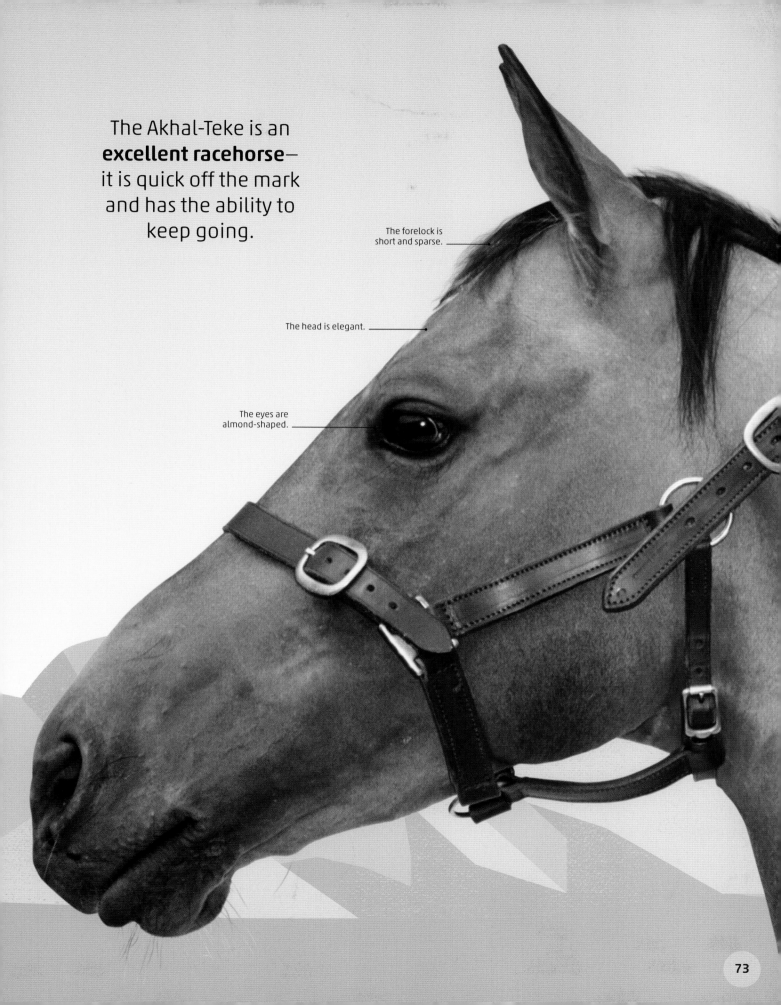

The Akhal-Teke is an **excellent racehorse**— it is quick off the mark and has the ability to keep going.

The forelock is short and sparse.

The head is elegant.

The eyes are almond-shaped.

Spotted horse
APPALOOSA

ORIGIN
United States

HEIGHT
14.2–15.2 hands
(147–157 cm)

COLOR
Spotted with various
coat patterns

There are **five main Appaloosa coat patterns**, and all are spotted.

One of the most popular American breeds, the Appaloosa is best known for its spotted coat—it has been bred for its spots as well as its tremendous stamina, hardiness, and calm temperament.

The origins of the Appaloosa are unclear. People had long thought that it was brought to North America by the Spanish in the late 15th and early 16th centuries. However, there is a more recent theory that the spotted horse may possibly have been brought to America from Asia much earlier. We do know that the indigenous Nez Percé people were breeding horses in the Pacific northwest region of the US in the 18th and 19th centuries. These horses have definite links to the Appaloosas of today. The name of the breed is derived from the Palouse River that ran through Nez Percé lands. The breed was almost lost in the 1870s, but interest in its revival began in the late 1930s, and the breed has since gone from strength to strength.

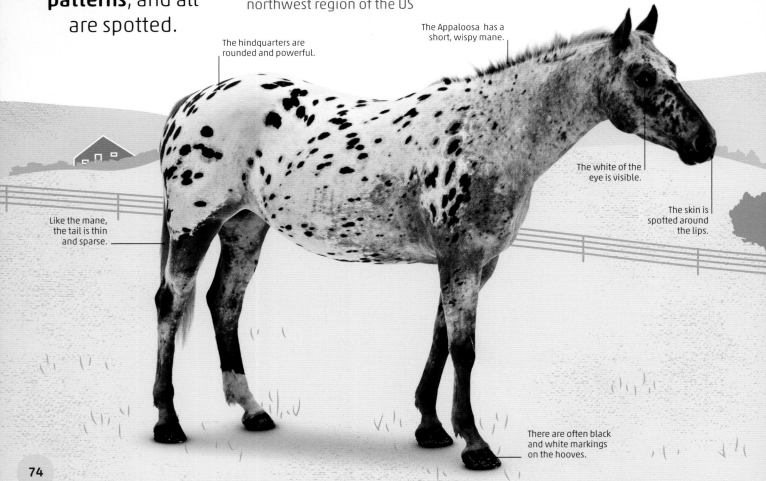

The Appaloosa has a short, wispy mane.

The hindquarters are rounded and powerful.

The white of the eye is visible.

The skin is spotted around the lips.

Like the mane, the tail is thin and sparse.

There are often black and white markings on the hooves.

Versatile horse
QUARTER HORSE

ORIGIN
United States

HEIGHT
15–15.3 hands
(152–160 cm)

COLOR
Usually chestnut but can
be any solid color

Quarter horses earned their name in the mid-17th century, when at the end of a day's work on the farm, they were regularly raced over a quarter of a mile. These horses are now a favorite at American rodeos and number in the millions.

Some believe the quarter horse to be the first American purebred horse. Its origins can be traced back to the 17th century, when European settlers crossbred Spanish, Barb, and Arab horses with imports from England. The resulting breed was fairly compact, with powerful hindquarters. It was fast, hard-working, and incredibly agile. Years of being bred to work

on the farm have made today's quarter horses supremely confident around cattle. The partnership between rider and horse also makes the work easier. As well as herding cattle, the breed has a variety of uses, including trail-riding, rodeo, and racing—quarter horse races can offer considerable prize money.

The heavily muscled hindquarters provide the driving power needed for short bursts of speed.

The neck is long, flexible, and muscular.

The head is short and broad, with a straight profile.

The muzzle is small.

The upper legs are heavily muscled.

The legs are lean and powerful.

The knees are wide and flat.

Over short distances, the quarter horse can reach a **top speed** of 55 mph (88 km/h).

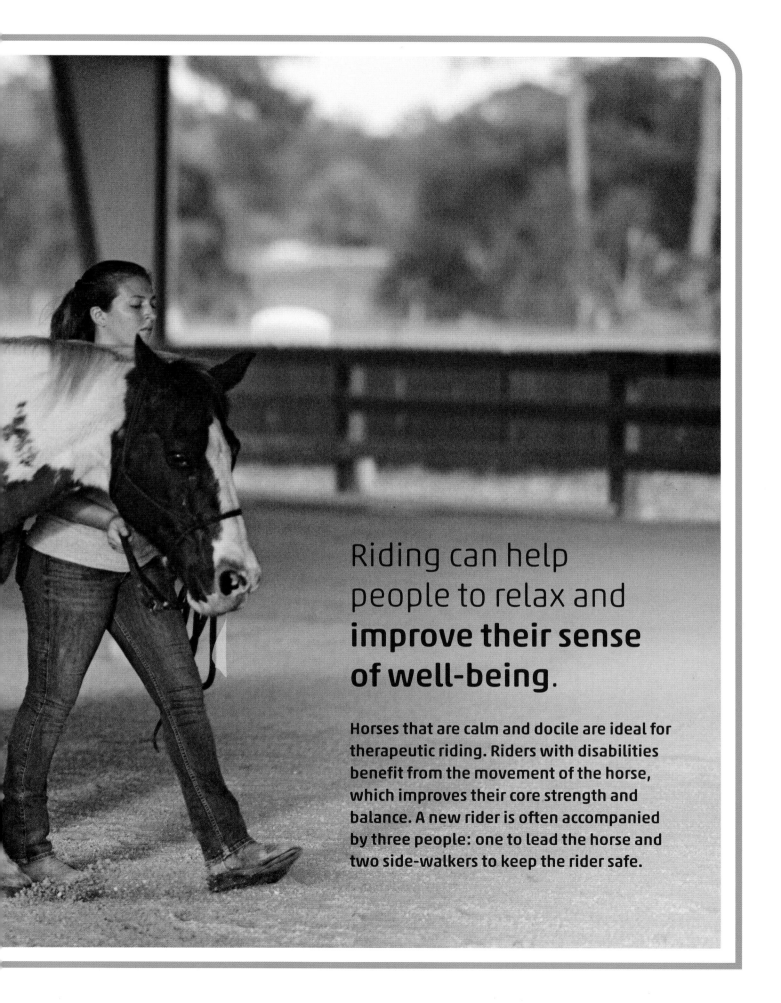

Riding can help people to relax and **improve their sense of well-being.**

Horses that are calm and docile are ideal for therapeutic riding. Riders with disabilities benefit from the movement of the horse, which improves their core strength and balance. A new rider is often accompanied by three people: one to lead the horse and two side-walkers to keep the rider safe.

Heavy horses

Gentle giant
SHIRE

ORIGIN
England

HEIGHT
More than 17 hands
(173 cm)

COLOR
Black, bay, brown,
or gray

This magnificent horse derives its name from the shires, or counties, in central England where it was once bred. During the 19th and early 20th centuries, Shires were a vital part of the workforce on farms and in factories, making light work of pulling plows and heavy carts.

Today, Shire horses are still used on a few small farms, but they are more often seen in horse shows, street parades, or plowing competitions. They are colossal horses—the tallest recorded horse was a Shire named Sampson, born in 1846. He reached 21.2 hands (219 cm) in height and was renamed Mammoth. Despite their size and strength, they are good-natured, gentle horses, which makes them very easy to handle, even when part of a team of horses. Over the years, their numbers have decreased, and they are now a rare breed— there are only about 1,500 Shire horses left in the world.

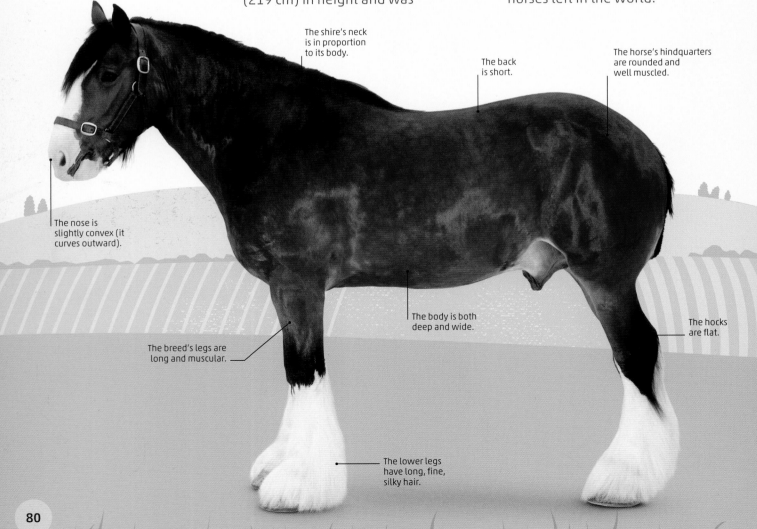

The shire's neck is in proportion to its body.

The back is short.

The horse's hindquarters are rounded and well muscled.

The nose is slightly convex (it curves outward).

The body is both deep and wide.

The hocks are flat.

The breed's legs are long and muscular.

The lower legs have long, fine, silky hair.

The Shire is
the **biggest and
most powerful**
horse in the world.

The Shire has a
long, broad head.

The tall and mighty Shire can **easily haul loads** of about three times its weight.

For centuries farmers used oxen to plow the land, but when the heavy horse collar was invented in the 12th century, it became possible to harness the Shire's immense power. The breakthrough invention meant the horse could use its strong hindquarters to push the load rather than pull it.

Horsepower
CLYDESDALE

ORIGIN
Scotland

HEIGHT
16.2–18 hands
(168–183 cm)

COLOR
Bay, brown, or chestnut;
can also be gray,
roan, or black

The Clydesdale has similar qualities to the English Shire breed—it is docile and powerful. During the early 1900s, its strength was put to good use by factory owners and farmers, who used this breed for pulling heavy carts through city streets and for plowing fields.

Clydesdales have been exported throughout the world, including to Germany, Russia, North America, and Australia. They were used in Canada and the US to plough the vast prairies, and in Australia, they are referred to as "the breed that built Australia." Clydesdales are bred to have hard-wearing hooves that are the size of dinner plates. Despite this, they have an elegant high-stepping gait. Most have a white blaze on the face and white markings on the legs.

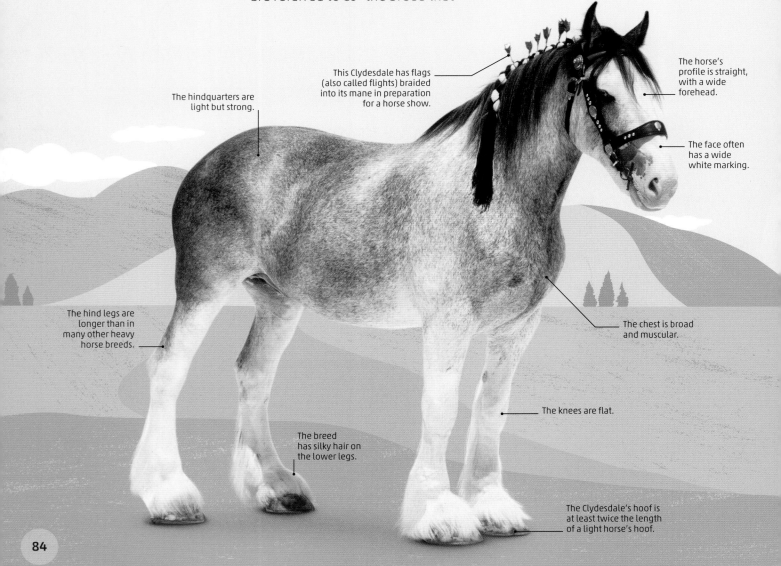

The hindquarters are light but strong.

This Clydesdale has flags (also called flights) braided into its mane in preparation for a horse show.

The horse's profile is straight, with a wide forehead.

The face often has a wide white marking.

The hind legs are longer than in many other heavy horse breeds.

The chest is broad and muscular.

The knees are flat.

The breed has silky hair on the lower legs.

The Clydesdale's hoof is at least twice the length of a light horse's hoof.

Versatile horse
IRISH DRAFT

ORIGIN
Ireland

HEIGHT
15.2–17 hands
(158–174 cm)

COLOR
Bay, grey, brown,
or chestnut

The Irish draft horse was bred to be both taller and more powerful than the native Irish ponies. A versatile breed, it was relied on for hundreds of years for doing farm work, for pulling the family carriage, and for riding.

Nowadays, the Irish draft is used for events and show jumping. Known for its willing nature and very calm temperament, it is also the perfect horse for police work, helping to patrol busy streets or control large crowds. The Irish draft is often crossed with other breeds, usually the Thoroughbred, to produce a horse known as the Irish sport horse. These horses are known for their cross-country and show-jumping skills. The demand for these excellent sport horses means that the pure Irish Draught breed is less popular.

The Irish draft horse has a wide forehead.

The neck is long and slightly arched.

The shoulders slope.

The hindquarters slope sharply.

This horse's tail has been braided for a show.

The body has a distinctive oval rib cage.

The breed has a leg-bone measurement of about 9 in (23 cm).

There is hardly any hair on the legs.

The **most senior animal** in the British army is a drum horse named Perseus.

The Household Cavalry helps to guard the British royal family, and takes part in ceremonial occasions. The Shire and the Clydesdale work as drum horses, and are chosen not only for their size and strength, but also for their calm attitude toward crowds and noise.

Pearl of the forest
BLACK FOREST HORSE

ORIGIN
Germany

HEIGHT
14.1–16 hands
(145–163 cm)

COLOR
Chestnut

Black Forest Horses may be small, but they are incredibly strong and hardy. They were once relied upon to haul timber out of the mountainous Black Forest region of southwest Germany and to do farm work. They have been bred in Germany for at least 200 years.

Black Forest Horses are among the world's most attractive horses—in the past, farmers referred to them as the "Pearls of the Black Forest." These horses are always chestnut with a flaxen mane and tail, but the chestnut ranges from pale to a shade so dark it can look black— in Germany, a horse with a dark coat and pale mane and tail is known as *dunelfuchs*, meaning "dark fox." Black Forest Horses are now mostly chosen for leisure riding and for pulling carriages. Thanks to their placid temperament and patient nature, they make ideal therapy horses, gently helping both children and adults to improve their coordination, balance, muscle strength, and sense of well-being.

The mane, which is the most distinctive feature, is thick, long, and slightly wavy.

The horse's hindquarters are heavily muscled.

The head is small and elegant.

The breed has a strong, muscular second thigh (known as the gaskin).

The Black Forest Horse has short legs in relation to the rest of its body.

There is very little hair on the lower legs.

The hoof is tough, which helps the horse to cope with the rugged terrain of the region.

Long strider
ITALIAN HEAVY DRAFT

ORIGIN
Italy

HEIGHT
15–16 hands
(152–163 cm)

COLOR
Mostly liver chestnut;
can be roan or chestnut

This breed's Italian name, *Tiro Pesante Rapido*, means "quick heavy draft" and reflects the breed's movement—these horses have a lively trot with long strides. The Italian heavy draft is still used by farmers in a few areas where farm machinery is not very practical.

These horses carry two brand marks, both on the left side of their body. They show a five-rung ladder within a shield and indicate the horse is a perfect example of the breed. The Italian heavy draft is smaller than other heavy horse breeds—a feature that was developed over time to meet the demand for a fast-moving but lighter heavy horse. A lighter horse is cheaper to keep, which makes it more suitable for smaller farms. It is also a very muscular breed with strong limbs and can maintain a good speed when hauling heavy loads.

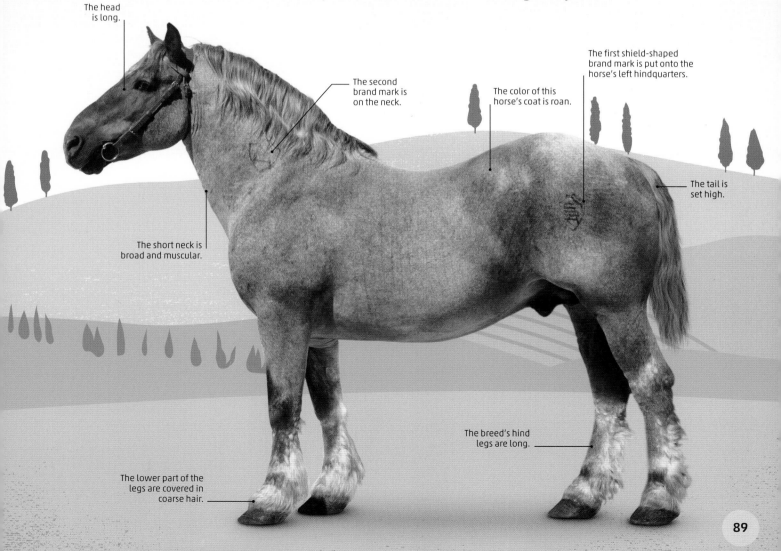

The head is long.

The second brand mark is on the neck.

The color of this horse's coat is roan.

The first shield-shaped brand mark is put onto the horse's left hindquarters.

The tail is set high.

The short neck is broad and muscular.

The breed's hind legs are long.

The lower part of the legs are covered in coarse hair.

Willing worker
PERCHERON

ORIGIN
France

HEIGHT
15-19 hands
(152-193 cm)

COLOR
Dapple gray; can also
be found in black, bay,
chestnut, or roan

This elegant heavy horse takes its name from the Perche district of northern France, where it has been bred for the past 200 years. An excellent all-rounder, it is a well-liked breed—it's thought that more Percherons are foaled today than any other draft breed.

The Percheron is a very adaptable breed. This is because of all the different qualities that it has inherited from crossbreeding with such horses as the elegant desert Arab horse or the tough South American criollo. A graceful, docile, and obedient breed, the Percheron is a popular choice for carriage work—it is often seen in shows and parades, including at Disneyland in California. Because of its easy-going nature, the Percheron is also an excellent riding horse.

In France, Percherons are divided into **petit** (under 16 hands) and **grand** (above 16 hands).

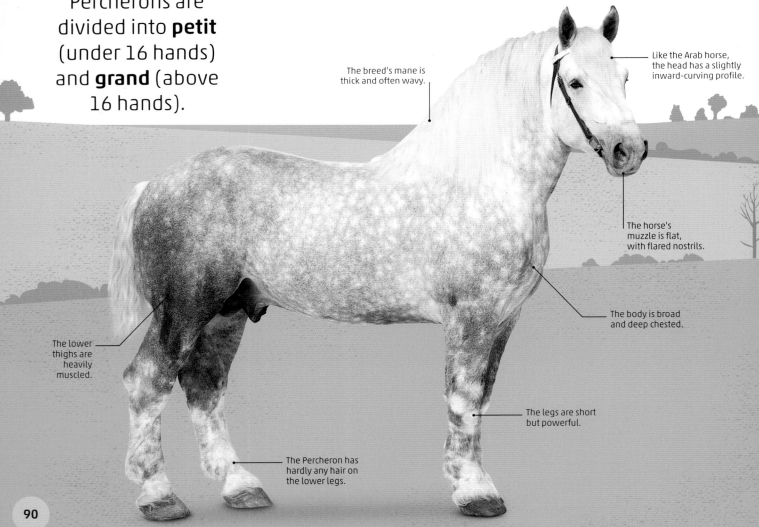

The breed's mane is thick and often wavy.

Like the Arab horse, the head has a slightly inward-curving profile.

The horse's muzzle is flat, with flared nostrils.

The body is broad and deep chested.

The lower thighs are heavily muscled.

The legs are short but powerful.

The Percheron has hardly any hair on the lower legs.

Slow and steady
DUTCH DRAFT

ORIGIN
Netherlands

HEIGHT
16 hands (163 cm)

COLOR
Chestnut, bay, or gray

The Dutch draft is sometimes called the Zeeland Horse, after the province in southwest Netherlands where it was first bred. It is a truly impressive horse and the heaviest of all the draft horse breeds in the Netherlands.

Draft horses in general are known for their easy-going, calm nature, and the Dutch draft is no exception. The breed is also known for its slow, steady movement and its ability to keep going. With its sturdy, muscular body and powerful legs, the Dutch draft made light work of plowing the heavy clay soil of the Netherlands and hauling logs. Today, although it can still be seen at work on small farms, the breed is mostly used as a carriage horse and in shows.

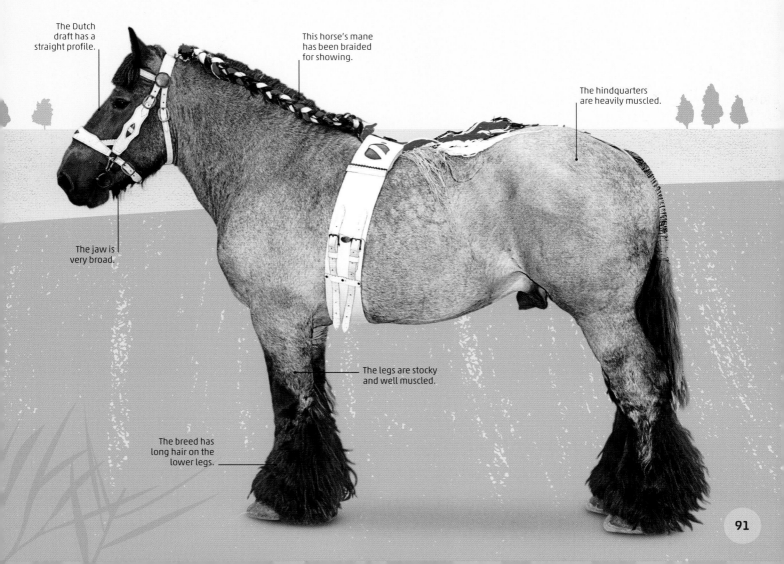

The Dutch draft has a straight profile.

This horse's mane has been braided for showing.

The hindquarters are heavily muscled.

The jaw is very broad.

The legs are stocky and well muscled.

The breed has long hair on the lower legs.

91

The Percheron is **a friendly giant** that can weigh more than a small car.

The powerful Percheron is strong enough to haul really heavy loads, and makes light work of pulling this sleigh. In the 19th century, Percherons were used to pull buses on the streets of Paris, France. The horses must trust each other and their driver to work as an efficient team.

The **world's tallest living horse** is a Brabant named Big Jake. He is 20.3 hands (210 cm).

The head is small and refined compared to other heavy breeds.

Tall and strong
BRABANT

ORIGIN
Belgium

HEIGHT
16.2–20.3 hands
(168–210 cm)

COLOR
Bay, black, or chestnut

Also known as the Belgian heavy draft, the Brabant dates back to the early 1600s. It is an important heavy horse breed, because it was used to develop other European breeds, including the Shire and the Clydesdale. The Brabant is still used as a working horse today.

The popular Brabant breed has been exported to many countries, including France, Germany, and Russia as well as the US, where they are the most common of all draft horses. It is a tall breed—two of the record holders for the world's tallest living horse, including the current holder, have been Brabant horses. In Belgium, these powerful animals are still a big part of such traditions as shrimp fishing on horseback—the horses pull the nets through shallow waters at low tide.

The mane and tail of this chestnut-colored horse are flaxen.

The Brabant's body is compact and powerful.

The neck is strong and held high.

The legs are short but very sturdy.

Many Brabant horses have white or lighter-colored socks.

The lower legs have some hair.

95

Horseback shrimp fishing on the coast of Belgium dates back hundreds of years.

In the town of Oostduinkerke in western Belgium, fishermen take to the sea on Brabants to catch shrimp. The horses drag long, funnel-shaped nets that vibrate to encourage the shrimp to jump up and into the nets. The catch is placed in large baskets that hang from each side of the horse.

Ponies

Small but strong
SHETLAND

ORIGIN
Scotland

HEIGHT
Up to 10.2 hands
(107 cm)

COLOR
Any color

Shetland ponies may be small, but they are exceptionally strong. They take their name from the Shetland Islands, their native home off the northern coast of Scotland. It is a harsh, windy, and wet environment, but the ponies have developed a resilient nature.

Small ponies have lived on the Shetland Islands for at least 4,000 years, having wandered across an ice bridge that once connected the islands to Europe. But the precise origin of today's breed is unknown. On their native islands, Shetland ponies were used to carry peat for fires and seaweed for fertilizer. In the 1800s, many were exported across the world to haul heavy loads in coal mines. Their size and strength made them ideal pit ponies, and they quickly adjusted to living underground. More recently, Shetland ponies have been used as riding ponies for young children. The breed's ability to adapt to different tasks has ensured its survival.

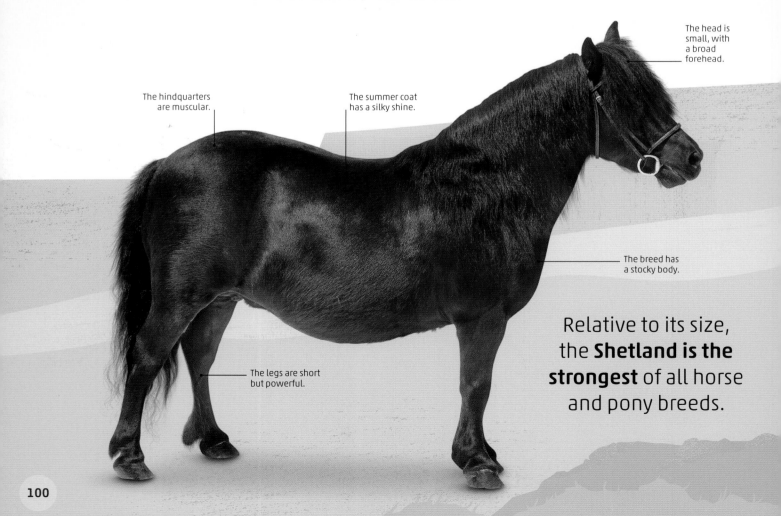

The head is small, with a broad forehead.

The hindquarters are muscular.

The summer coat has a silky shine.

The breed has a stocky body.

The legs are short but powerful.

Relative to its size, the **Shetland is the strongest** of all horse and pony breeds.

Moorland pony
EXMOOR

ORIGIN
England

HEIGHT
12.2–12.3 hands
(127–130 cm)

COLOR
Bay, brown, or dun

Exmoor is a large expanse of moorland in the southwest of England. The Exmoor breed has lived on this moorland for hundreds of years, managing to survive in this remote habitat, where grazing can be poor during the cold winter months.

The Exmoor breed is the oldest and purest of Britain's 16 native horse and pony breeds. Ponies were recorded roaming Exmoor in the Domesday Book—the survey of England ordered by William the Conqueror in 1085. The breed is believed to have grazed there ever since. The Exmoor is a short, stocky pony, with a muscular neck.

As well as having a double-layered winter coat, it has "toad eyes"—fleshy eyelids that help to protect the eyes from the cold, wet weather. It also has a distinctive pale banding around the eyes as well as on the muzzle and the underbelly—a feature it may have inherited from ancient wild horses.

Pale hair surrounds the eyes.

The Exmoor pony has a compact body with a fairly level back.

The thick tail protects the hindquarters from rain and snow.

The muzzle is always a lighter color.

The underbelly is a lighter color.

The hind legs are short and strong.

The Exmoor pony has black leg markings.

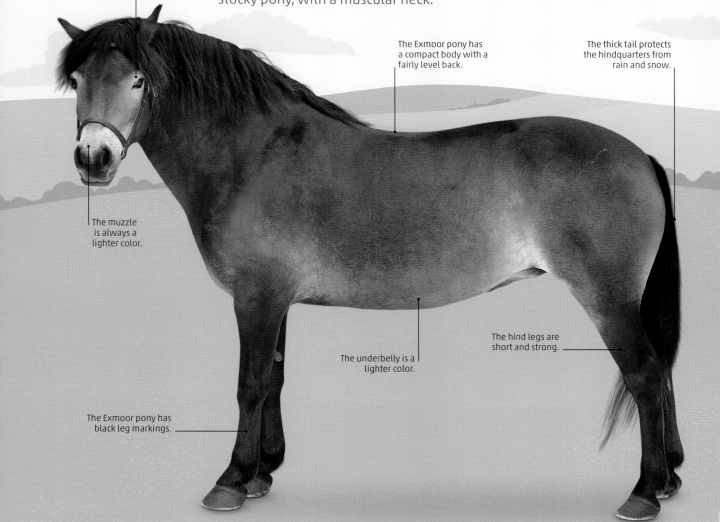

The Shetland grows a **thick double coat** to survive the harsh winter months.

In the Shetland Islands, north of Scotland, temperatures fall to an average low of 37°F (2°C) in midwinter, but biting winds make it feel colder. A Shetland pony's winter coat has a thick, woolly underlayer that provides warmth and an oily topcoat that directs rain to run off the animal. They don't mind the cold or the wet weather!

Show pony
RIDING PONY

ORIGIN
England

HEIGHT
12.2–14.2 hands
(127–147 cm)

COLOR
Any solid color

All over the world, children take their riding ponies to compete in shows such as dressage, show jumping, and eventing. Riding ponies fall into three categories: show ponies, show hunter ponies, and sports ponies.

The riding pony has its origins in polo, an equestrian sport in which two teams of riders compete to hit a ball with long-handled mallets. In the 1850s, there was a growing demand for a small but beautiful horse to be used for polo. Breeders then realized that these ponies could be bred for other purposes and so the riding pony was developed—a small, graceful, good-looking pony for the show-ring. It is the result of crossing ponies with small Thoroughbreds as well as Arab horses. The outline of the riding pony resembles that of a mini Thoroughbred and it also has the same elegant proportions and flowing movement.

The long shoulders slope.

The pony's back is strong but short.

The tail is set fairly high.

The veins on the head are visible through the thin skin.

The riding pony is the most **perfectly proportioned** pony.

The breed has a well-developed gaskin (also known as a second thigh).

The pony has broad, flat knees.

Pony perfection
WELSH MOUNTAIN PONY

ORIGIN
Wales

HEIGHT
12 hands
(up to 122 cm)

COLOR
Any solid color

The Welsh Mountain pony has often been called the most beautiful of all British ponies. A hardy, brave, and friendly breed, it has been exported all over the world, and is an outstanding children's riding pony.

Like all British mountain and moorland ponies, Welsh ponies came under threat about 500 years ago when King Henry VIII of England ordered that all ponies under 15 hands living on common land be destroyed. King Henry didn't see the point of a horse that couldn't carry a knight in full armor. Fortunately, many ponies survived, including the hardy ponies that even then could be found in the Welsh mountains. Today, there are four types of Welsh pony and they are divided into sections. They have much in common with each other but also have their own characteristics.

The ears are small and pointed.

The small head tapers to the muzzle.

The pony's hindquarters are compact and powerful.

The Welsh Mountain pony's neck is long and lean.

The breed's legs are slender but sturdy.

The hooves are round and small.

The Welsh Mountain pony is the **oldest and smallest** of the four types of Welsh pony.

105

Horse of the Vikings
ICELANDIC

ORIGIN
Iceland

HEIGHT
13-14 hands
(132-142 cm)

COLOR
All colors, but chestnut
is common

Although the Icelandic horse is the size of a pony, it is always referred to as a horse by Icelanders. It was first brought to Iceland by Viking settlers in the 9th century and has played an important role in the lives of local people.

The tough Icelandic horse is one of the world's purest horse breeds—Iceland's government forbids the import of horses and has done so since 982 CE, which has helped preserve the breed's purity. Sure-footed in all weathers, the Icelandic horse is known for its five gaits—the ways that it moves at certain speeds. These are walk, trot, canter/gallop (seen as one gait for Icelandic horses), tölt, and flying pace.

The tölt is a fast-paced movement that is very comfortable for long rides. The flying pace is faster and is used in racing—it's an unusual gait in which both legs on one side of the horse move together. The Icelandic horse can reach a speed of about 30 mph (48 km/h) in flying pace, almost as fast as a Thoroughbred racehorse at full gallop.

The Icelandic horse has a straight profile.

The thick mane gives the horse some protection against the cold weather.

The coat grows thicker in winter and sheds in warmer months—shown here is the horse's summer coat.

The shoulders are upright and help contribute toward the horse's elevated gaits.

The legs are short but very strong.

Chestnut Icelandic horses have a white or flaxen (pale yellow) mane and tail.

To ensure the **purity of the breed**, an Icelandic horse that is taken abroad for competitions can't be brought back into its native country.

Icelandic horses **return home from their summer retreat** in time for winter.

Every autumn, hundreds of Icelandic horses are brought down from the highlands where they have roamed freely over the summer. The largest round-up takes place in the Kolbeinsdalur Valley, where the owners welcome back their horses and celebrate bringing them safely home before winter closes in.

Top-class pony
CONNEMARA

ORIGIN
Ireland

HEIGHT
12.2-14.2 hands
(127-148 cm)

COLOR
Gray, black, bay, brown, or dun but can also be roan, chestnut, palomino, or cream

This hardy, elegant pony used to roam the mountains and moorlands of Connemara in the west of Ireland. It is the island's only native pony. Once put to work by farmers, it can now be seen competing successfully in the sporting world.

Ponies have existed in Ireland for thousands of years and it is thought that Spanish horses were imported to breed with the Connemara's ancestors. Farmers relied on the hard-working Connemaras to pull plows across fields and to haul seaweed from the coast, which was then used as a fertilizer to improve the land. Nowadays, Connemaras make excellent sporting ponies, competing in show jumping, endurance riding, and dressage. Connemaras are intelligent, quick, brave, and agile. They are also good-natured ponies, and so are perfect for young riders.

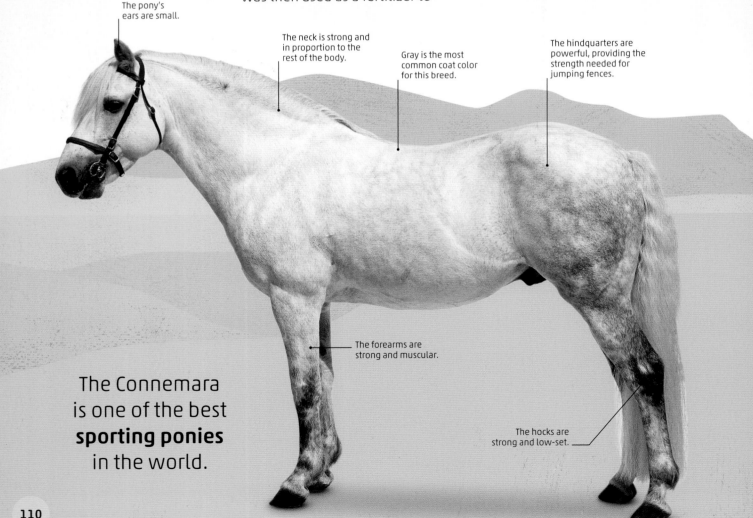

The pony's ears are small.

The neck is strong and in proportion to the rest of the body.

Gray is the most common coat color for this breed.

The hindquarters are powerful, providing the strength needed for jumping fences.

The forearms are strong and muscular.

The hocks are strong and low-set.

The Connemara is one of the best **sporting ponies** in the world.

Rare breed
SORRAIA

ORIGIN
Portugal

HEIGHT
14–14.2 hands
(142–147cm)

COLOR
Dun or grulla (tan-gray)

The Sorraia takes its name from the region where it once roamed—between the Sor and Raia Rivers that run through Portugal. It is a primitive-looking breed—with its coloring and markings, it resembles the horses shown in ancient cave paintings.

In the past, Sorraia ponies helped farmers round up cattle, but with the increasing use of machines on farms in the 1900s, the demand for these exceptionally hardy ponies fell. They were left to roam in the wild, living off what little food they could find. On the brink of extinction, the ponies were saved by a Portuguese zoologist, Dr. Ruy d'Andrade, who kept a small breeding herd on his land. Although there are now a few herds in Germany as well as Portugal, the breed remains endangered, with only about 200 ponies left. Sorraia ponies tend to vary in temperament: they can be calm and easy to train, but others maintain a strong independent spirit.

The tail is held low and close to the body.

There is a dark stripe along the back and sometimes across the neck and shoulders.

The Sorraia has a striking two-tone mane and tail.

The ear tips are black.

The long head has a slightly convex (outward-curving) profile.

The pony's face and muzzle are darker than the rest of the body.

The legs are long and straight with dark markings.

The hooves are often black.

Surefooted pony
FJORD

ORIGIN
Norway

HEIGHT
13–14 hands
(132–142 cm)

COLOR
Dun

The unusual looking Fjord pony has survived in Norway for thousands of years. Ponies resembling the Fjord were depicted in Viking art and so it is likely that these ponies were used by the Vikings for riding and for pulling heavy loads.

The Fjord's most striking feature is its mane, which is traditionally cut so that the dark hair at the center stands out. The Fjord pony also has a dark stripe along its back, a feature the breed may have inherited from its primitive ancestors. An incredibly hardy, surefooted pony, the Fjord is quite used to the mountainous terrain of its habitat as well as the bitterly cold climate. It is a docile breed and has tremendous strength and stamina—it can still be seen at work on a few remote farms, plowing the land or carrying heavy loads. It also makes a good children's riding pony.

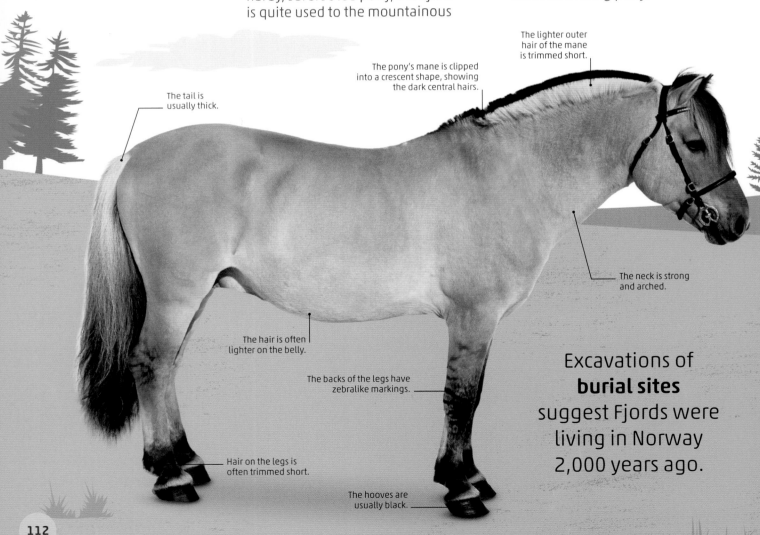

The lighter outer hair of the mane is trimmed short.

The pony's mane is clipped into a crescent shape, showing the dark central hairs.

The tail is usually thick.

The neck is strong and arched.

The hair is often lighter on the belly.

The backs of the legs have zebralike markings.

Excavations of **burial sites** suggest Fjords were living in Norway 2,000 years ago.

Hair on the legs is often trimmed short.

The hooves are usually black.

Woodland horse
GOTLAND

ORIGIN
Sweden

HEIGHT
11.1-12.3 hands
(115-130 cm)

COLOR
Dun, black, bay,
or chestnut

This tough breed has lived on the small Swedish island of Gotland since the Stone Age. It is thought to be the oldest Scandinavian breed and is Sweden's only native pony. In Gotland, it is known as the *Skogruss*, which means "little horse of the woods."

These ponies once roamed freely on the island, where they were left to forage for food on moorland and in woods. A few farmers also kept herds, using them for farm work and carrying goods. But as more land was fenced off and farmed in the early 1900s, the ponies were seen as pests. Many were exported to other countries, where they were used as pit ponies (put to work deep underground in coal mines). Today, semiferal herds still live on the island, where they are protected by the local people. Because Gotland ponies are very athletic and quick, they are perfect for show jumping and trotting races.

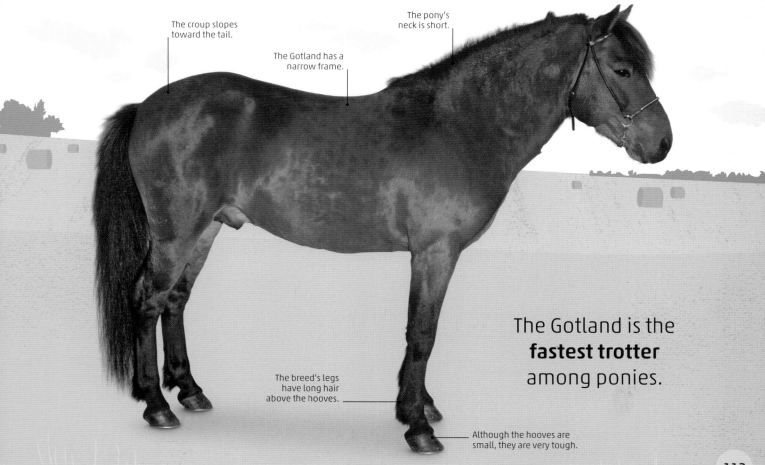

The croup slopes toward the tail.

The Gotland has a narrow frame.

The pony's neck is short.

The breed's legs have long hair above the hooves.

Although the hooves are small, they are very tough.

The Gotland is the **fastest trotter** among ponies.

The mane is very thick.

The Hokkaido's head is large in relation to its body.

About **75 percent** of Japan's native horses and ponies are **Hokkaido ponies.**

Tough survivor
HOKKAIDO PONY

ORIGIN
Japan

HEIGHT
12.3–13.1 hands
(130–135 cm)

COLOR
Mostly solid colors

This resilient breed is named after the Japanese island of Hokkaido and is also known in Japan as *Dosanko*, which means "born in Hokkaido." It is taller than most of Japan's eight native breeds and the only one that is not endangered.

Hokkaido ponies are believed to have evolved from horses that fishermen introduced to the island of Hokkaido in the 17th and 18th centuries to help haul their catches of herring. The horses were left on the island to survive the winter months alone, in a mountainous habitat with scarce food. Those that survived, largely on bamboo grass, were put to work again by the returning fishermen the following spring. Over time, the breed became incredibly hardy. Today, most roam freely on the island in large grazing areas and farmers still use them for transportation and farm work. As in the past, they are released to fend for themselves in the mountains during the winter months, helping to maintain the breed's hardiness.

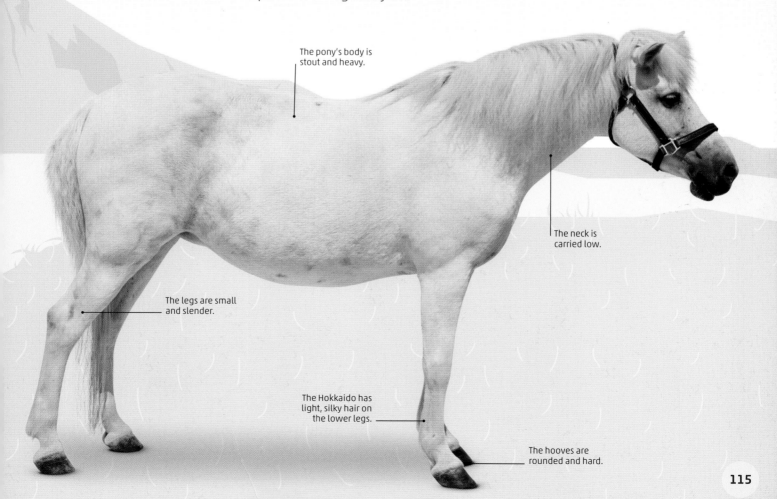

The pony's body is stout and heavy.

The neck is carried low.

The legs are small and slender.

The Hokkaido has light, silky hair on the lower legs.

The hooves are rounded and hard.

Horses in Mongolia **live in the open** where stables are rare.

Mongolian horses may have descended from Japanese Hokkaido ponies. They are tough enough to cope with bitterly cold weather and long rides with little to eat or drink. Tack is often handmade, with the bridles knotted together.

Island pony
SUMBA

ORIGIN
Indonesia

HEIGHT
12.2 hands (127 cm)

COLOR
Mostly solid colors

The Sumba takes its name from an island in an archipelago (a large group of islands) between Java and Timor in Indonesia. However, these ponies are found throughout the Indonesian islands. They may be descended from ponies that once lived in landlocked central Asia.

Sumba ponies are very important to the islands because they can access areas that are hard to reach by vehicle. They are strong, willing riding ponies—although they are small, they can easily carry an adult. The ponies are swift and surefooted, making them an excellent choice for bareback races as well as the national sport of pasola—a wooden spear throwing competition between two groups of riders. The ponies are also used in traditional Indonesian dance ceremonies, in which they are decorated with brightly colored ribbons, flowers, and bells.

The mane is very thick.

This pony's dun coat color is typical of the breed.

The breed has a distinctively large head in relation to the body.

The neck is short and muscular.

The breed's legs are short but strong.

The lower legs are dark.

Sumbas are ridden with **braided leather bridles** that are identical to those used in central Asia about 4,000 years ago.

Show-ring pony
AUSTRALIAN PONY

ORIGIN
Australia

HEIGHT
12–14 hands
(122–142 cm)

COLOR
Any solid color

The graceful-looking Australian pony is known for its gentle nature and smooth, long strides. These features have made it a popular children's pony in its home country as well as an outstanding show pony.

Australia has no native ponies— the horses and ponies there have all been introduced from other countries during the past 250 years. The first nine horses were shipped over from South Africa in 1788 by early settlers. There are now 10 breeds, including the Australian pony. The elegant Australian pony has been influenced by a number of breeds, including the Welsh Mountain pony, the Thoroughbred, and the Arab.

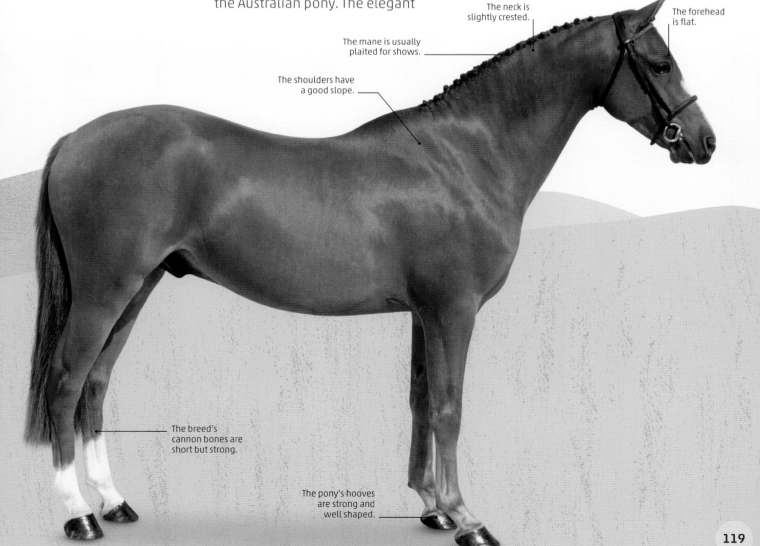

The neck is slightly crested.

The forehead is flat.

The mane is usually plaited for shows.

The shoulders have a good slope.

The breed's cannon bones are short but strong.

The pony's hooves are strong and well shaped.

Sumba horses take part in Indonesia's **popular annual festival**—the Pasola.

Hundreds of people gather in the fields in February and March to celebrate the start of the rice-planting season. The Pasola festival involves two teams competing on horseback in a mock battle. These days, the riders carry blunt sticks instead of the sharp, metal-tipped spears used in the past.

Spotted pony
PONY OF THE AMERICAS

ORIGIN
United States

HEIGHT
11.2–14 hands
(117–142 cm)

COLOR
Spotted

The eye-catching Pony of the Americas was bred specifically for its spots. Like the Colorado ranger and Appaloosa breeds, also from the US, it has one of five spotted coat patterns—leopard, frost, snowflake, blanket, and marble.

The first Pony of the Americas, bred from a Shetland stallion and an Arabian-Appaloosa mare, was born in 1954. It had a white coat with black spots, and one of the markings looked like a hand print, so the foal was named Black Hand. The owner went on to set up the Pony of the Americas Club and the breed was born.

The pony is a good choice for young riders, as it is narrower in the body than many other ponies. This makes it more comfortable for children to sit on, and easier for their legs to reach the stirrups. It is also an affectionate pony and quick to learn.

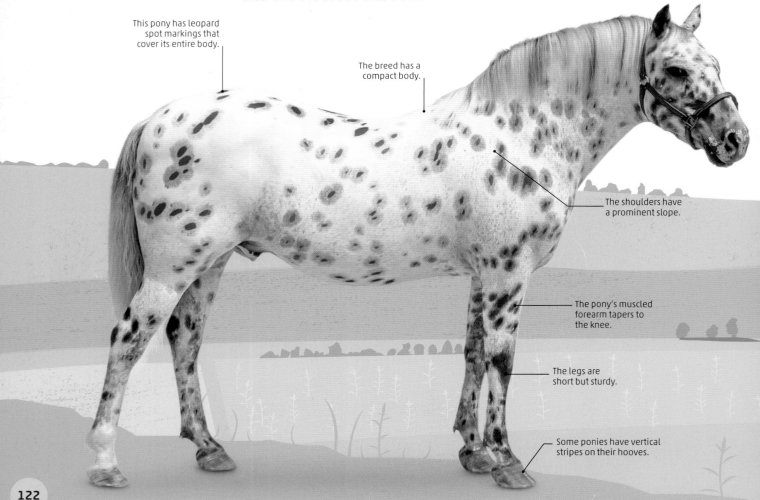

This pony has leopard spot markings that cover its entire body.

The breed has a compact body.

The shoulders have a prominent slope.

The pony's muscled forearm tapers to the knee.

The legs are short but sturdy.

Some ponies have vertical stripes on their hooves.

The Pony of the Americas
is **one of only three
spotted horse and pony
breeds** in the US.

The skin is mottled
on the horse's muzzle.

Spanish roots
GALICEÑO

ORIGIN
Mexico

HEIGHT
12–13.3 hands
(122–140 cm)

COLOR
Any solid color

These fast-moving ponies are descended from Spanish horses brought to the island of Cuba and then Mexico in the 16th century. They are known for their smooth running walk, where they take long strides and cover a lot of ground quickly.

Galiceño ponies are tough, quick, and obedient with tremendous stamina. They were ridden by Mexican farmers for hundreds of years and are still relied upon for light work on the farm and for carrying goods. In the 1950s, a herd of 135 was exported to Texas, where the ponies were prized for their agility and quickness and put to good use in rounding up cattle. They were also seen as a good riding pony for children. Today, despite the fact that some are still used for cattle work in the US as well as for riding and show jumping, Galiceños are an endangered breed.

Galiceño ponies have distinctive pointed ears that are hooked at the tip.

The pony's back is short and straight.

The nostrils are crescent-shaped.

The neck is held upright.

This horse's coat color is palomino.

The well-defined legs have flat knees.

The Galiceño takes its name from the northwestern **Spanish province of Galicia**, where its ancestors originated.

124

Tiny in size
FALABELLA

ORIGIN
Argentina

HEIGHT
8.3 hands
(up to 89 cm)

COLOR
Any color

The Falabella is named after the Argentinian family who first developed the breed in the 19th century. Its size makes it a pony but the Falabella is often described as a miniature horse. It is a hardy, long-lived breed with a gentle, friendly nature.

In the 1850s, a miniature-horse herd was developed in Argentina from a selection of small local ponies. Later, small Thoroughbreds and Shetlands were introduced. Other breeds were added to the mix to produce the Falabella's spotted markings. But the quest to produce a near-perfect miniature horse caused a number of weak points in the offspring. For instance, the Falabella's legs and hindquarters aren't as strong as the Shetland's. Despite this, the Falabella is still a popular breed. Its tiny size makes it a perfect riding horse for small children, though it is too weak to carry older children or adults. On the other hand, while most horses live for between 20 and 30 years, the Falabella can live well into its 40s.

The Falabella is the **world's smallest** breed of horse and pony.

This Falabella's spotted coat is one of many patterns found in this breed.

The hindquarters are weak.

The head is in proportion to the body.

The tail is thick and bushy.

The front half of the horse is bulky.

The hind legs are not very strong.

Horse care

Some horses are clever enough to undo bolts, so a horse-proof bolt at the top of the base door prevents the horse from escaping if the kick over bolt is not in place.

WINDOW

A window provides a good source of light and ventilation. If glazed, a transparent plastic sheet is ideal as well as a wire mesh protective covering. The covering prevents the horse from chewing on the window frame.

KICK OVER BOLT

The bolt at the bottom of the stable door is called the kick over bolt. It can be knocked into place with your foot and holds the door securely shut. If your hands are full, a kick over bolt is particularly useful.

The stable

Many horses are stabled for some of the time, either overnight or for long periods during the day when they can't be out in a field. A stable needs to be a safe, comfortable area for a horse. Although stables vary in how they look, the basic features are the same.

SPLIT DOORS

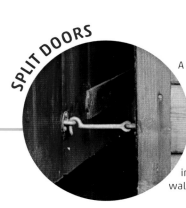

A stabled horse can become bored. All stables have split doors so the top door can be left open to allow the horse to look out and see what's going on. The door should always be held back on a hook so it doesn't swing around and injure the horse or people walking by.

A stable or loose box should look out onto a yard—or be grouped with other stable boxes.

YARD FLOOR

The area outside the stable box should always be kept clean. Any loose straw or dung can make the area slippery. The floor should also be a hard floor instead of a dirt floor to keep the area from becoming muddy.

WHAT'S INSIDE?

Essentially, a horse must be able to move around freely in the stable as well as be able to lie down on a comfortable bed. But a stable also needs to contain a few other horse-care essentials.

WATER BUCKET
Horses need a constant supply of fresh water, and stabled horses drink from buckets. A loose bucket can be kicked over, so a hook holds it securely to the wall. Buckets with a flat side can then be hung against the wall.

TIE RINGS
All stables have metal rings. They are needed for tying a horse's lead rope to when tacking up, grooming, or checking a horse's hooves. Always tie a horse to string on a ring, and never directly to the ring, so that if the horse panics and pulls back the string will break.

MANGER
In a field, a horse will happily spend the day eating grass. However, a stabled horse needs food and this is sometimes given in a manger. It is attached to the wall to make it more comfortable for the horse to eat.

A large American barn might have stables for **30 or more horses**.

American barns are usually built from timber, and allow many horses to be housed under one roof. Stables lie on either side of a central passageway. When inside, the horses can keep an eye on each other—horses like company.

Food and water

Both wild and domestic horses eat little and often throughout the day. Grass and hay are called "roughage"—together they make up the bulk of a horse's diet. In the wild, horses spend about 60 percent of their time eating grass, or "grazing." Domestic horses have a more varied diet—in addition to roughage, they also eat oats, ready-mixed feeds, and the occasional healthy snack.

THE DIGESTIVE SYSTEM

Horses are specially adapted for eating and digesting grass. Grass has a low nutritional content so horses must eat huge amounts to get all the nutrients they need. Compared to humans, horses have a much bigger cecum—a pouch between the small and large intestines. Bacteria in the cecum break down tough plant fibers before turning them into sugar, which gives the horse energy.

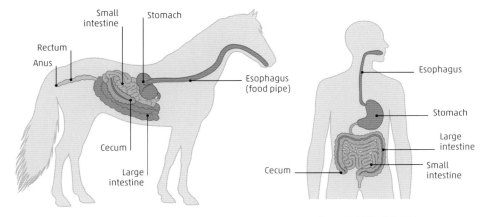

A HORSE'S DIGESTIVE SYSTEM
A horse has a small stomach because it feeds little and often. Its cecum is much bigger than a human's, even in relation to its bigger size.

A HUMAN'S DIGESTIVE SYSTEM
Humans have larger stomachs in relation to their body size than horses, but their cecum is much smaller, as they have no need to digest grass.

GRAZING IN A FIELD

Horses feed on pasture—areas of land with grass and plants that are suitable for eating. While out on the pasture, they spend their time grazing, then snoozing, before moving to a different spot to graze a bit more. It's important to keep a pasture clear of horse droppings and of plants that may make horses sick.

WATER

Horses need constant access to clean water. Each day a healthy horse needs to drink between 8 and 12 gallons (36 and 55 liters)—that's as much as five and a half buckets of water.

HAY

Along with grass, hay makes up the bulk of a horse's diet. Hay is dried grass—it's greenish brown in color and crispy in texture. Hay must be stored in a dry place to prevent mold.

OATS

Many horses are fed grains such as oats, in addition to grass and hay. Oats are easy to digest and contain lots of fiber, which gives the horse energy. Most horses love eating oats.

READY-MIXED FEEDS

Mixtures of grains and pellets are given to horses doing lots of work or exercise, as they need extra food for energy. The mixture given is specially chosen based on a horse's nutritional needs.

SALT

In the wild, many animals obtain essential minerals by licking naturally occurring salt deposits. A block of salt, called a salt lick, is the best way to give salt to a domestic horse.

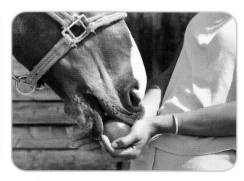

HEALTHY SNACKS

Nearly all horses enjoy getting snacks—they're usually given one or two apples and a few carrots a day. Some large horses can eat apples whole, but most people cut them into smaller pieces.

Mucking out

From mucking out the stable, to changing bedding, and sweeping the yard, cleaning is a big part of caring for a horse and keeping it healthy. Stables must be mucked out every day to prevent any risk of infection from dirty bedding materials. When cleaning a stable, it's best for the horse to be kept elsewhere for a short while, so that they don't get in the way.

TOOLS

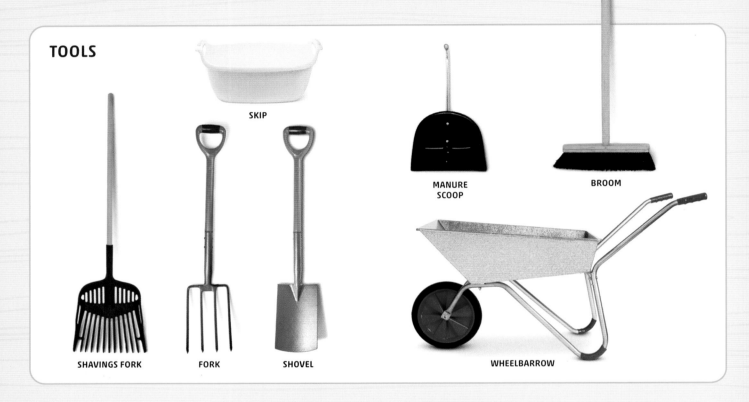

SKIP

MANURE SCOOP

BROOM

SHAVINGS FORK

FORK

SHOVEL

WHEELBARROW

BEDDING MATERIALS

A stabled horse needs a clean, comfortable bed. There are lots of bedding materials to choose from, each with its own pros and cons. Straw is traditional, but horses can suffer from allergies just like people, and straw dust can cause them breathing difficulties. Some horses like to eat their straw bedding so their keepers use an alternative, such as hemp or wood shavings.

STRAW

Straw is comfortable for most horses and usually cheap.

Hemp, made from the hemp plant, absorbs a lot of moisture.

HEMP

Shredded paper or cardboard can be heavy to lift when wet.

SHREDDED PAPER

Shavings are more absorbent than straw and good for horses with breathing difficulties.

WOOD SHAVINGS

MUCKING OUT BEDDING

If a horse stands in dirty bedding, it can lead to infections in the feet, as well as other illnesses. So a stable should be mucked out every day, which means removing all droppings and any wet bedding.

REMOVE THE DROPPINGS

Step 1

Use a fork to lift out any droppings you can see. It's best to lift out a little bit of straw with each forkful. If there aren't many droppings, they can be removed by putting them into a skip.

A plastic basket like this one can be used as a skip.

SORT THE BEDDING

Step 2

Next, separate the dirty straw from the clean material. If there is a lot to get rid of, load it into a wheelbarrow.

Move the dirty straw into a pile, making it easier to remove.

SWEEP THE FLOOR

Step 3

Once you've piled all the clean bedding to one side, sweep the floor clear of any remaining dirty straw so you can remove it. Always take dirty straw straight to a muck heap.

Leave the floor as clean as possible.

PUT DOWN NEW BEDDING

Step 4

Use a fork to lay fresh, clean bedding. If you are laying straw, you need to break it up before laying. Mix the older bedding in, leaving it higher at the sides of the stable.

Use the fork to toss the straw into the air to fluff it up.

MUCKING OUT SHAVINGS

Different types of bedding need to be mucked out in different ways. When dealing with shavings, it's easier to use a shavings fork and scoop as shavings are less bulky than straw.

REMOVE THE DROPPINGS

Step 1

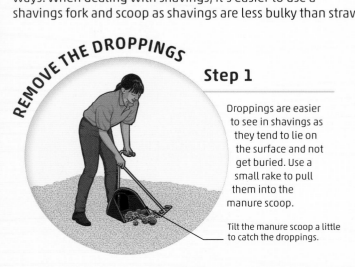

Droppings are easier to see in shavings as they tend to lie on the surface and not get buried. Use a small rake to pull them into the manure scoop.

Tilt the manure scoop a little to catch the droppings.

ADD FRESH SHAVINGS

Step 2

Next, use the shavings fork to sift through the shavings for any missed droppings and wet areas. Remove these with a shovel. Finally, add in fresh shavings and level the bed out, but leave the sides higher.

Grooming a horse

A stabled horse needs to be groomed daily. Grooming helps to keep the horse's skin healthy and its coat free of mud. It also allows you to look for any signs of injury or disease. For a horse, it is a relaxing experience—some will even doze off while they are groomed.

GROOMING EQUIPMENT

Each horse in a stable should have its own kit, which helps to prevent the spread of disease. The equipment in the grooming kit depends on the horse—if a horse has a thick winter coat, it will need brushes that have longer, stiffer bristles. If a horse has its summer coat, or is clipped, it will need softer brushes.

WATER BRUSH

A water brush is for brushing stains off the horse's body. It can also be used to dampen the mane and tail before braiding the hair for a show or riding competition.

SPONGES

When grooming, you need two damp sponges—one to gently clean the horse's nose and eyes, and the other for the area under the base of its tail, known as the dock. You should never mix up these sponges and always clean them after use.

GROOMING KIT

Keep your grooming kit together in a waterproof box so you have everything you need to hand. Always make sure you clean your brushes and sponges—it's hard to clean a horse when your equipment is dirty.

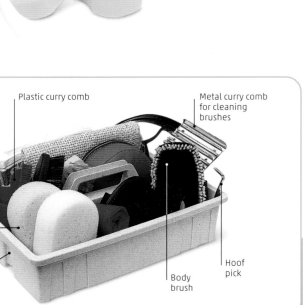

Plastic curry comb

Metal curry comb for cleaning brushes

Sponges

Plastic tray for storing grooming kit

Body brush

Hoof pick

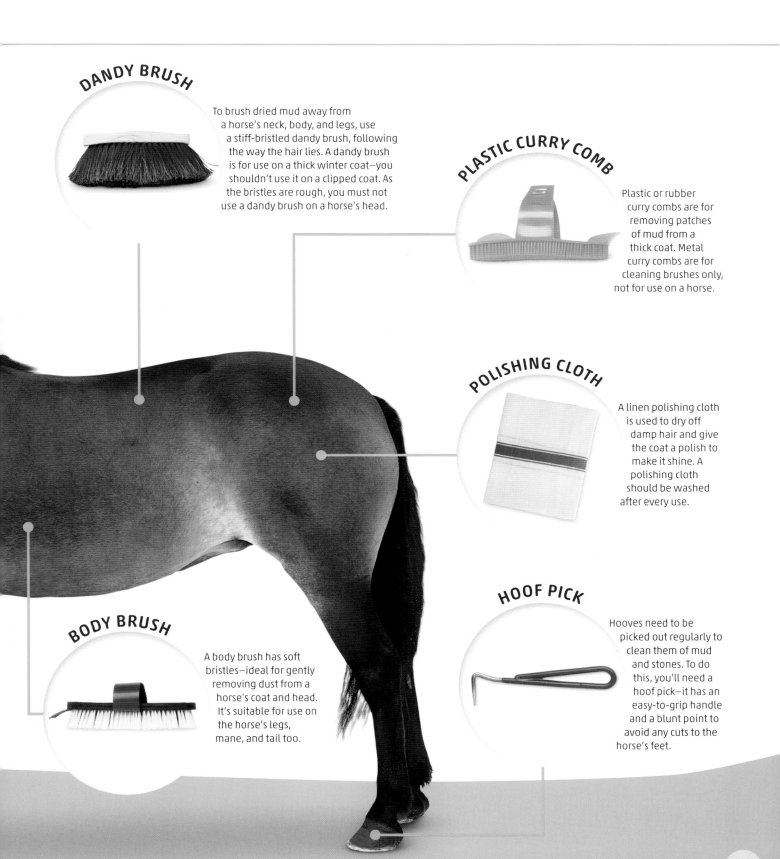

DANDY BRUSH

To brush dried mud away from a horse's neck, body, and legs, use a stiff-bristled dandy brush, following the way the hair lies. A dandy brush is for use on a thick winter coat—you shouldn't use it on a clipped coat. As the bristles are rough, you must not use a dandy brush on a horse's head.

PLASTIC CURRY COMB

Plastic or rubber curry combs are for removing patches of mud from a thick coat. Metal curry combs are for cleaning brushes only, not for use on a horse.

POLISHING CLOTH

A linen polishing cloth is used to dry off damp hair and give the coat a polish to make it shine. A polishing cloth should be washed after every use.

BODY BRUSH

A body brush has soft bristles—ideal for gently removing dust from a horse's coat and head. It's suitable for use on the horse's legs, mane, and tail too.

HOOF PICK

Hooves need to be picked out regularly to clean them of mud and stones. To do this, you'll need a hoof pick—it has an easy-to-grip handle and a blunt point to avoid any cuts to the horse's feet.

REMOVE THE OLD SHOE

Step 1

A shoe is held on with nails. When a shoe needs replacing, it is removed with pincers. Most horses learn to stand patiently while a blacksmith works.

Using pincers, the blacksmith carefully removes the worn shoe.

FILE THE HOOF

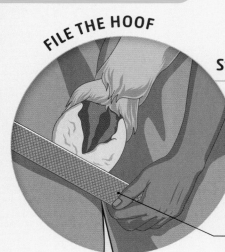

Step 2

Once the old shoe is off, the hoof wall is filed to remove any uneven surfaces. This is known as "rasping" and doesn't hurt the horse. The metal rasp is like a huge nail file.

The hoof is filed so that it is ready for the new shoe.

MAKE A NEW SHOE

Step 3

Horseshoes have to be shaped to fit. This is done by heating the shoe so the metal can then be hammered into the correct shape.

The heated horseshoe is shaped around an anvil.

CHECK FOR SIZE

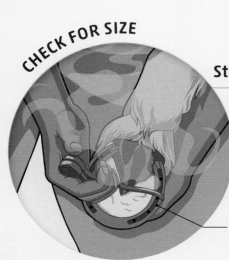

Step 4

The blacksmith holds the hot shoe against the hoof. This reveals any raised areas of that hoof that need a little more rasping to make the hoof level.

The new shoe is gently held against the hoof to discolor any raised areas.

Shoeing

NAIL ON THE SHOE

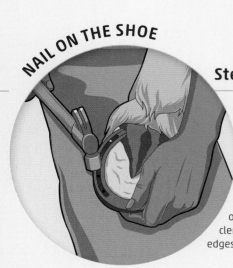

Step 5

When the shoe is ready, it is cooled in a bucket of water and then attached with nails. The ends of the nails that appear through the hoof wall are twisted off and bent over to become clenches. Any sharp edges are rasped away.

Like your hair or fingernails, a horse's hooves grow continuously. But if a horse is regularly ridden, the hooves may wear down too quickly, and this can cause problems. To protect the hooves, most working horses are fitted with iron shoes. A specially trained person called a blacksmith checks the horses' hooves every four to six weeks.

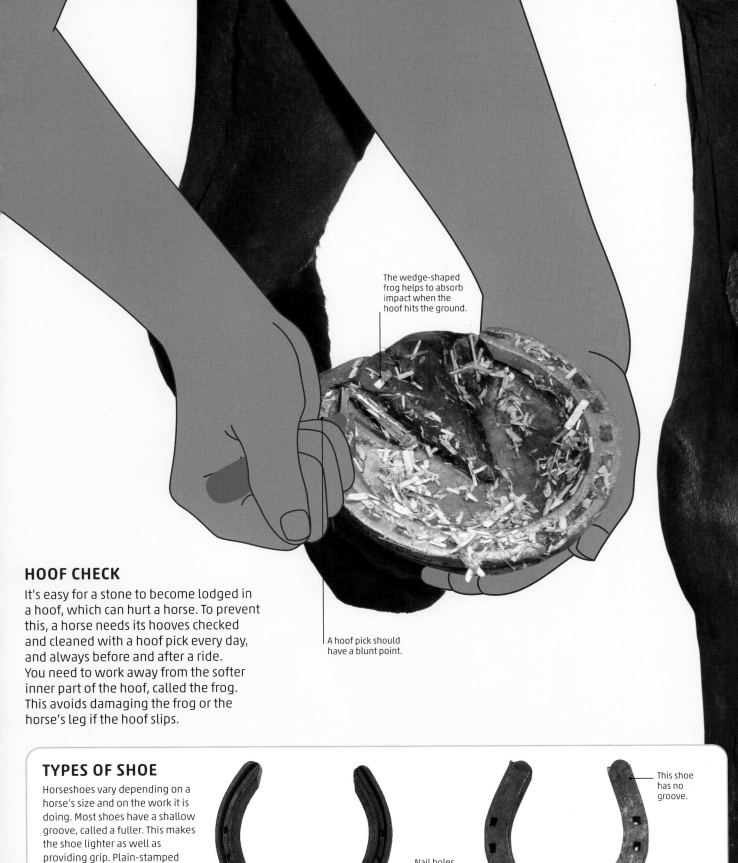

The wedge-shaped frog helps to absorb impact when the hoof hits the ground.

A hoof pick should have a blunt point.

HOOF CHECK

It's easy for a stone to become lodged in a hoof, which can hurt a horse. To prevent this, a horse needs its hooves checked and cleaned with a hoof pick every day, and always before and after a ride. You need to work away from the softer inner part of the hoof, called the frog. This avoids damaging the frog or the horse's leg if the hoof slips.

TYPES OF SHOE

Horseshoes vary depending on a horse's size and on the work it is doing. Most shoes have a shallow groove, called a fuller. This makes the shoe lighter as well as providing grip. Plain-stamped shoes have no groove. They are good for horses that are doing slow-paced farm work and don't require as much grip.

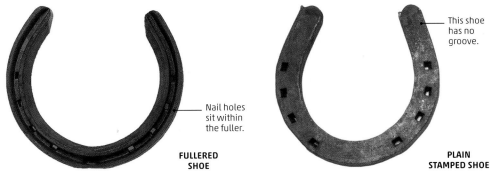

This shoe has no groove.

Nail holes sit within the fuller.

FULLERED SHOE

PLAIN STAMPED SHOE

Staying healthy

From vet check-ups to vaccinations, there are many ways to keep a horse healthy. It's much better to keep horses in good condition and take simple steps to keep them from getting ill than it is to treat them if they get sick. If a horse is ill or hurt, its eyes or coat may appear dull in color and it might behave differently.

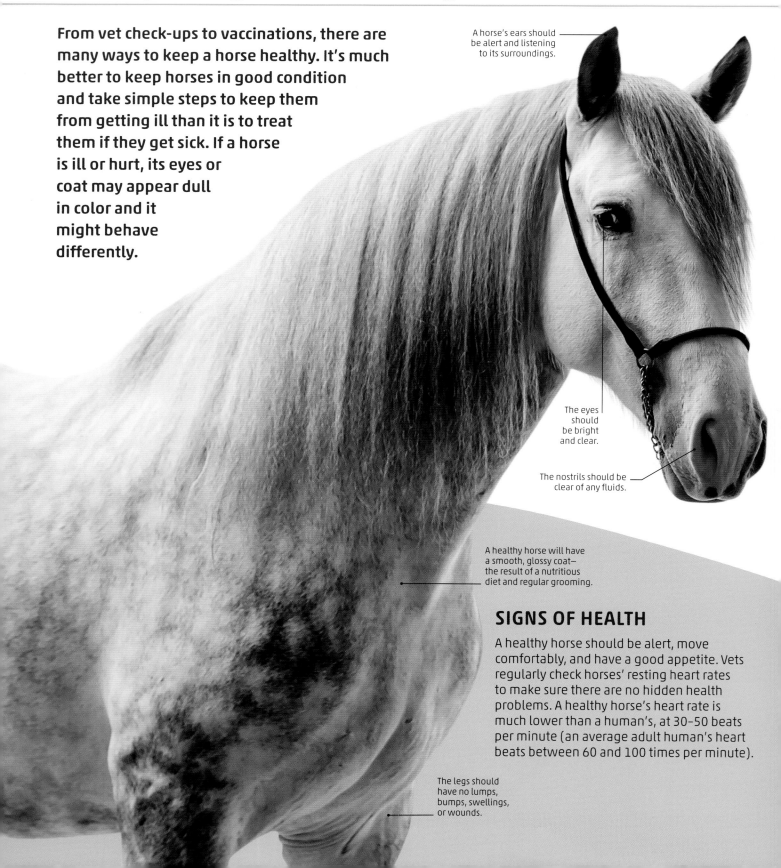

A horse's ears should be alert and listening to its surroundings.

The eyes should be bright and clear.

The nostrils should be clear of any fluids.

A healthy horse will have a smooth, glossy coat—the result of a nutritious diet and regular grooming.

SIGNS OF HEALTH

A healthy horse should be alert, move comfortably, and have a good appetite. Vets regularly check horses' resting heart rates to make sure there are no hidden health problems. A healthy horse's heart rate is much lower than a human's, at 30–50 beats per minute (an average adult human's heart beats between 60 and 100 times per minute).

The legs should have no lumps, bumps, swellings, or wounds.

VACCINATION

Vets protect horses from a range of diseases by injecting them with vaccines (treatments to produce resistance to specific diseases). How often a horse needs to be vaccinated depends on how widespread a disease is locally.

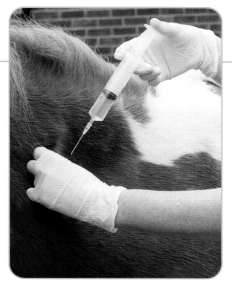

WORMING

Worms can get into and grow inside the large intestine of horses, making them feel unwell. To keep a horse from becoming infected with worms, a syringe of worming liquid is squeezed into the back of its mouth on a regular basis.

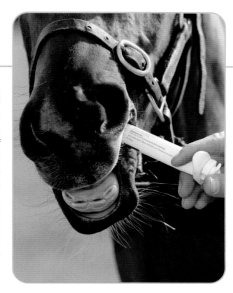

DENTAL CARE

A horse's teeth are constantly being worn down by chewing and may develop sharp edges, which can hurt or make it hard for the horse to eat. During a check-up, a horse dentist grinds away these sharp edges, a process called "rasping."

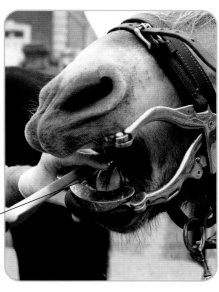

Special equipment is used by the dentist to hold the horse's mouth open.

WOUND CARE

Most horses get a minor wound, such as a cut, at some point in their lives. It's important to check regularly for wounds and clean and treat any you find immediately. Applying a bandage helps to stop any bleeding by putting pressure on the wound.

TEETH AND AGE

A horse's teeth keep growing throughout the horse's life to make up for wear caused by chewing food. It means that it's possible to roughly tell a horse's age just by looking at its teeth. The more angled the front teeth are, the older the horse is.

A young horse's teeth are fairly straight.

Galvayne's groove appears.

As the tooth has grown, Galvayne's groove has moved.

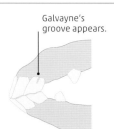
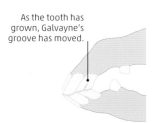

5 YEARS OLD
By the age of five, a horse's milk teeth have been replaced by permanent teeth, which are reasonably straight.

10 YEARS OLD
By 10 years old, its teeth have begun to slope. A brown mark known as "Galvayne's groove" appears on two of the front teeth.

25 YEARS OLD
An older horse's teeth are angled forward. The top teeth are longer than the bottom ones, which have been ground down.

NECK AND BELLY CLIP

This clip has the hair on the neck, chest, and belly removed in one long strip. These are areas where the horse will sweat heavily, so the neck and belly clip is ideal for horses doing light work.

BLANKET CLIP

This clip leaves a "blanket" of hair over the horse's back, and keeps hair on the legs for extra warmth. It's the best type of clip for horses that are ridden regularly.

CHASER CLIP

The chaser clip keeps the muscles of the neck and back warm by leaving the coat in place there. It's ideal for horses doing fast work where they may also be left standing still in the cold.

WHICH CLIP?

Choosing the right clip for a horse depends on many different factors, such as the horse's age, how often it's outside, how much work it does, and even how much it sweats.

A clip begins at the shoulder, moves up the neck and down the body, and finally to the head and legs, if needed.

This horse has a hunter clip.

Clipping a horse

Each winter, a horse's coat grows thicker to ensure it stays warm in the cold. Horses used for riding and working can get hot and sweaty if their coats are too thick. So to keep them comfortable in winter, they are a given a "clip" (haircut).

An area of the back is left unclipped to protect the skin from any rubbing when the horse wears a saddle.

Hair is left on the legs to help keep them warm.

TRACE CLIP

In a trace clip, the hair on the head is left on or only partly removed to give extra warmth and protection. The line of the clip from front to back can be higher or lower depending on what type of work the horse does.

HUNTER CLIP

This clip keeps the legs warm and the saddle area protected. A horse with the hunter clip will need to wear an all-in-one rug when it's not being ridden to prevent it from getting cold.

FULL CLIP

The entire coat is clipped short in the full clip. It starts at the shoulder and works up the neck, then over the body, and then the head and legs. This clip is only suitable for a horse that is stabled throughout the cold winter months.

143

Rugs

Some horses may need to wear clothes: coats (called rugs), masks, sheets, and boots. Older horses or horses that have been clipped often need a rug to keep them warm, particularly in the winter. A horse may need a fly sheet and mask to protect it from insects in the summer.

Adjustable straps fit around the horse's belly.

COOLER RUG

Just like us, horses sweat when they get hot—and that sweat can chill them as they cool off. Cooler rugs allow a horse to dry off without getting cold—they are often thrown over a clipped horse after heavy exercise or after a bath.

FLY RUG

Some horses do not cope well with flies and other insects. Horses can have allergic reactions to insect bites—one example is sweet itch, which causes itching and hair loss. A fly rug helps to protect such horses, while also shielding them from the sun.

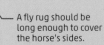

A fly rug should be long enough to cover the horse's sides.

PROTECTION

FLY MASK
A fly mask keeps flies from settling around a horse's eyes, and some masks cover the ears and nose as well. The mask's mesh is light to allow the horse to see through it.

TRAVELING BOOT
Sometimes horses are taken to shows in a horsebox. Strap-on boots provide extra padding to help protect their legs from possible knocks on the journey.

This boot is fastened on with straps.

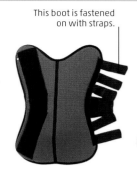

FRONT BOOTS IN PLACE

ALL-IN-ONE TURN OUT RUG

An all-in-one rug is both water- and windproof, and is used when putting a horse into a field, when it may need extra protection from the weather. Straps around the horse's belly and its hind legs help to keep the rug in place.

An exercise sheet is held in place by the saddle and girth, and by a fillet string under the tail.

EXERCISE SHEET

Sheets such as this are useful for keeping a clipped horse warm if it is used for slow work. Exercise sheets similar to this in shape but far lighter and made of wool are commonly used on racehorses before an early morning gallop.

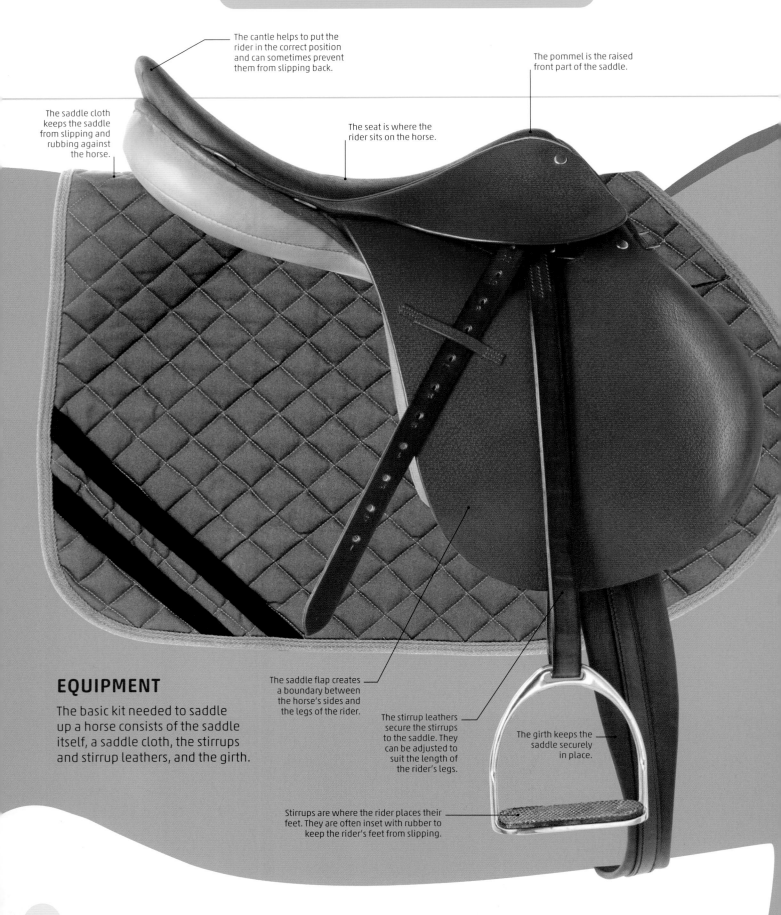

The cantle helps to put the rider in the correct position and can sometimes prevent them from slipping back.

The pommel is the raised front part of the saddle.

The saddle cloth keeps the saddle from slipping and rubbing against the horse.

The seat is where the rider sits on the horse.

EQUIPMENT

The basic kit needed to saddle up a horse consists of the saddle itself, a saddle cloth, the stirrups and stirrup leathers, and the girth.

The saddle flap creates a boundary between the horse's sides and the legs of the rider.

The stirrup leathers secure the stirrups to the saddle. They can be adjusted to suit the length of the rider's legs.

The girth keeps the saddle securely in place.

Stirrups are where the rider places their feet. They are often inset with rubber to keep the rider's feet from slipping.

Saddle up

A well-fitted saddle provides a comfortable seat for the rider and spreads weight evenly across the horse's back. A saddle is kept in place on the horse by a girth (a piece of leather or fabric that passes under the belly). Always clean off any dirt, dry mud, or sweat from the horse before placing a saddle and girth on it.

SADDLE CLOTH

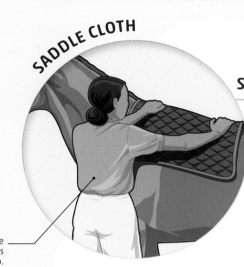

Step 1

Put the saddle cloth on the horse well in front of where the saddle will eventually sit. This will allow you to move it and the saddle back together later.

Keep close to the horse while it is tied up.

EASE IT ON

Step 2

Check that the stirrups are "run up"—pulled to the top of their leathers so that they don't hang below the saddle. The girth should be fastened to the right-hand side of the saddle and folded back up over the saddle. Lift the saddle and place it gently down onto the cloth.

PERFECT POSITION

Step 3

Using both hands, hold the saddle cloth close to the pommel and cantle of the saddle. Then move both the saddle and saddle cloth backward until the saddle sits in its correct position just behind the shoulder.

Grip the saddle and cloth at the pommel and cantle.

BUCKLE UP

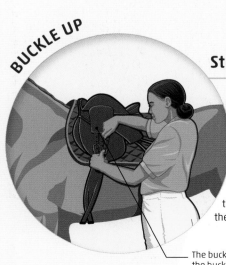

Step 4

Put down the girth and check that everything is flat. Walk back around and fasten the first and third straps of the girth. Move the buckle guards over the buckles of the girth. The guards help keep the buckles from damaging the saddle flaps.

The buckle guard lifts up while the buckles are adjusted.

REMOVING THE SADDLE

A horse should have its saddle removed when the ride is over. First, run the stirrups up the leathers, threading the leathers through the stirrups. Undo the girth on the left side and place it over the saddle. Then lift the saddle and saddle cloth off the horse.

Slide the saddle slightly back as you lift it off.

Types of saddle

When riders first start to learn, they sit on an all-purpose saddle as this is approriate for most types of riding. There are many other types of saddle, however, each suited to different types of riding—a racing saddle, for example, has a very different purpose than a western saddle.

ICELANDIC

Made for the small Icelandic horse breed, this saddle is positioned farther back on the horse and designed to provide for the breed's two special gaits—known as the tölt and the flying pace.

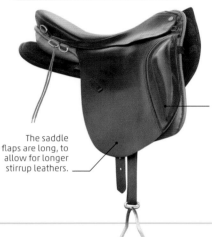

A knee roll helps maintain the rider's position.

The saddle flaps are long, to allow for longer stirrup leathers.

DRESSAGE

A dressage rider sits tall in the saddle, aiming for a straight line from the shoulder to the heel. A dressage saddle's long saddle flaps and high cantle help the rider to achieve this position.

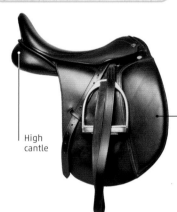

High cantle

The saddle flap is cut to be long and straight.

FLAT RACING

A jockey rises out of the saddle when racing, with the knees held forward. The saddle accommodates this, with flaps that are cut in front of the pommel. There is no padding.

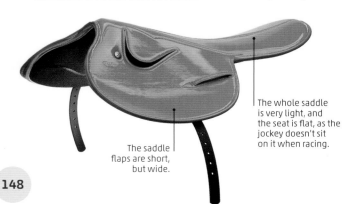

The saddle flaps are short, but wide.

The whole saddle is very light, and the seat is flat, as the jockey doesn't sit on it when racing.

SIDESADDLE

The sidesaddle has a long history, but is now largely seen at country shows and displays. The rider always sits with their legs over the horse's left shoulder, supported by a pair of pommels.

Pommel designed for the rider's top leg

The capped stirrups are designed to allow the foot to pull out of the stirrup in case of a fall.

EXTRA PADDING

SADDLE CLOTH
Saddle cloths are made from cotton or wool. They absorb sweat and help to keep the bottom of the saddle clean.

NUMNAH
Like the saddle cloth, the numnah absorbs sweat, and can also help to protect the horse's back.

GEL PAD
Pads can help a horse with a sore back as they distribute the pressure of the saddle more evenly.

POLICE SADDLE
Mounted police officers still operate in some cities, patrolling on horseback. While there is a lot of variation between them, these saddles are designed to be lightweight, but comfortable for rider and horse.

Extra tack and equipment can be attached to the saddle if needed.

WESTERN
This is a heavy saddle, designed for comfort given the long hours a cowboy can spend in the saddle. It is also strong enough to be able to withstand roping hefty cattle.

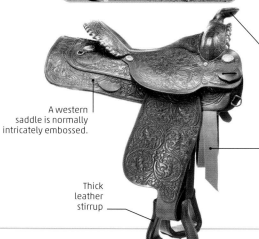

The horn is used to hold the rope when the rider is roping cattle.

A western saddle is normally intricately embossed.

The latigo attaches to the cinch, which passes around the horse's belly.

Thick leather stirrup

SHOW JUMPING
Show jumpers need saddles that provide a secure seat when a horse takes a high jump. The saddle flap is rounded at the front, to allow the rider to move their legs forward when the stirrups are shortened for jumping.

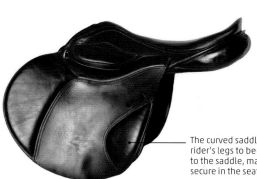

The curved saddle flaps allow the rider's legs to be positioned closer to the saddle, making the rider more secure in the seat.

POLO
A polo rider is constantly rising in the saddle and leaning down to hit a ball with a mallet. A polo saddle is therefore designed to sit a little farther forward than other saddles.

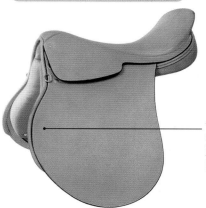

The saddle flaps are long, with a slight curve at the front to cushion the knee during play.

Decorative saddle rugs are placed above and below the saddle.

Every summer in the city of Lhasa, East Asia, crowds gather at the Sho Dun Festival to watch riders perform daring acrobatic stunts on horseback. Their saddles are made of wood, so colorful rugs are used to make them more comfortable for both horse and rider.

Putting on a bridle

A bridle can be fitted before or after the saddle. Always make sure that your horse can't wander away while you are tacking up. Slip the halter off your horse's nose, making sure it remains securely fastened around the neck so the horse can't move away while you are putting the bridle on.

SECURE THE HORSE

Step 1

First make sure that the bridle's noseband and throatlatch are undone, then stand on the horse's left side and slip the reins over the horse's head with your right hand. Once you've done this, adjust the halter so it is around the horse's neck.

The lead rope should be tied to string on a ring on the stable wall.

POSITION THE BRIDLE

Step 2

Grip the bridle in your right hand just under the browband. Hold it in front of the horse's face, with your right arm under the horse's neck. Pop your left thumb into the corner of the horse's mouth and ease the bit into the mouth.

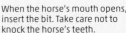

When the horse's mouth opens, insert the bit. Take care not to knock the horse's teeth.

PLACE THE HEADPIECE

Step 3

Don't let the bit slip out of the horse's mouth while you bring the headpiece up and over the horse's ears. The ears lie between the headpiece and the browband. Gently pull the forelock to lie over the browband.

CHECK AND FASTEN

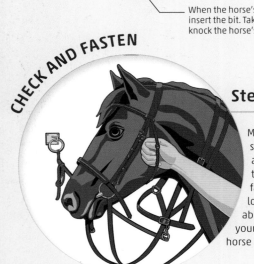

Step 4

Make sure that all the straps are lying flat as it's easy to get them twisted. Then fasten the throatlatch loosely. You should be able to fit the width of your hand between the horse and the throatlatch.

FASTEN THE NOSEBAND

Step 5

Fasten the noseband. A cavesson noseband, as here, lies under the cheekpieces and sits a little way above the bit. You should be able to fit two fingers between the nose and the noseband.

A bit should sit at the back of the horse's mouth.

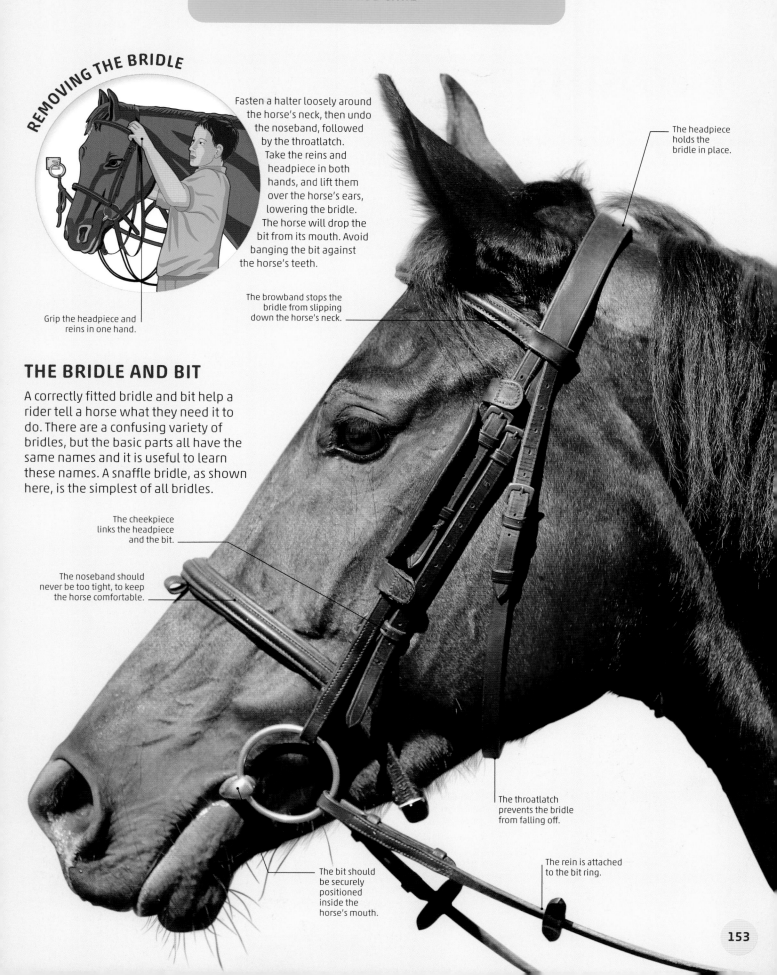

REMOVING THE BRIDLE

Fasten a halter loosely around the horse's neck, then undo the noseband, followed by the throatlatch. Take the reins and headpiece in both hands, and lift them over the horse's ears, lowering the bridle. The horse will drop the bit from its mouth. Avoid banging the bit against the horse's teeth.

Grip the headpiece and reins in one hand.

THE BRIDLE AND BIT

A correctly fitted bridle and bit help a rider tell a horse what they need it to do. There are a confusing variety of bridles, but the basic parts all have the same names and it is useful to learn these names. A snaffle bridle, as shown here, is the simplest of all bridles.

The headpiece holds the bridle in place.

The browband stops the bridle from slipping down the horse's neck.

The cheekpiece links the headpiece and the bit.

The noseband should never be too tight, to keep the horse comfortable.

The throatlatch prevents the bridle from falling off.

The rein is attached to the bit ring.

The bit should be securely positioned inside the horse's mouth.

Looking after tack

In the same way that your clothes need regular washing to keep them clean, tack also needs to be wiped down each time it's used. If tack isn't cleaned regularly, mud and grease can build up on it and damage the leather or rub against the horse's skin during riding.

CLEANING EQUIPMENT

SADDLE SOAP   STIFF BRUSH   SPONGE   BUCKET

DAMP CLOTH   POLISHING CLOTH   DRY CLOTH

CLEANING A LEATHER BRIDLE

A leather bridle should be cleaned thoroughly and treated with saddle soap each time it is used. As you're cleaning the bridle, check it carefully for any worn stitching. It should also be fully taken apart once a week to check for any torn leather or loose stitching—it might break while you're riding and could cause an accident.

HANG IT

Hang the bridle at eye level.

Step 1

Hang up the bridle so you can work through each of the straps in turn. Start by wiping down each strap with a damp, folded cloth. Rub each strap several times, rinsing the cloth regularly.

SOAP IT

Step 2

Saddle soap keeps leather supple. Always remember to moisten the saddle soap first, not the sponge, and then rub the sponge on the soap. Avoid using too much soap—a little goes a long way.

RUB IT

Step 3

Rub both sides of the bridle's leather straps with the sponge. Pay special attention to the area around the holes and buckles—dirt collects here and can cause the leather to dry out.

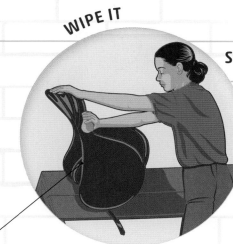

WIPE IT

Step 1

The easiest way to clean a leather saddle is to rest it on a saddle horse. Lift the saddle and use a damp sponge to wipe down the underside first, then wipe over the top.

CLEANING A LEATHER SADDLE

Before cleaning a leather saddle, remove the girth and the stirrup leathers. When you raise a saddle to clean its underside, always lift it onto its front, or pommel.

Lift the saddle to balance it on its front.

SOAP IT

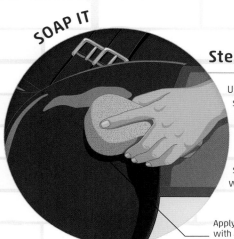

Step 2

Use a sponge to rub saddle soap into the leather areas of the saddle. Avoid any areas made from cloth or suede—these should be cleaned with a brush, not soap.

Apply the saddle soap with a circular motion.

PUT IT BACK TOGETHER

Step 3

Wipe the stirrup leathers over first, then use a sponge and saddle soap. Use the polishing cloth to remove any excess soap. Finally, reassemble the saddle, reattaching the girth and stirrup leathers.

THE STIRRUPS AND BIT

The best way to clean the stirrup irons is to remove them from the stirrup leathers, soak them in warm water, and then wipe them clean with a dry cloth. A bit needs washing every time it is used. When you rinse off the bit, avoid putting the leather straps into the water.

Try to keep the leather out of the water as this will damage it.

Soak the stirrup irons and bit in water to clean them.

Brush the girth in the direction of the grooves.

THE GIRTH

If the girth isn't made of leather, it will need a good brush to clean off the mud and grease. It can then be washed in warm, soapy water. Always rinse it thoroughly before hanging it up to dry.

THE HALTER

The horse's halter is in three parts: a headpiece that goes behind the horse's ears, the noseband, which is placed around its nose, and the cheekpieces that connect the two parts.

TAKE THE LEAD

Once the halter is attached to the horse or pony, lead it away quietly. Stay alert when leading it back to the stable yard, as it may try to pull away suddenly.

A well-fitted halter and lead rope is the safest way to lead a horse to or from the field.

The lead rope is attached to the halter with a metal clip.

Coming back in

Horses with the freedom to roam in a field can't stay outside all of the time. They will need to be caught for riding or taken to the stable. Some horses respond to a person's voice and will stand still if approached, but others will be so excited to have a visitor that they'll walk straight over!

HOW TO CATCH A HORSE

When entering a field where the horse is kept, make sure you close the gate after you. Once you reach the horse's shoulder, slip the lead rope around its neck and hold onto the rope as you put on the halter. Try not to make any sudden movements while you put on the halter.

SLOW APPROACH
To catch a horse, approach it slowly and calmly from the front, using your voice to say hello. Bring your halter with the lead rope with you and unbuckle the halter before slipping it over your shoulder. As you get closer to the horse, keep the halter behind your shoulder, out of sight.

FASTEN THE BUCKLE
A halter buckles on the left-hand side, once you've passed the headpiece over the top of the head, behind the horse's ears. Keep talking to your horse as you do up the buckle. Once that's done, lead the horse back to the stable yard, walking on the horse's left.

WHAT KNOT?

A quick release knot is the safest way to tie your horse up. Never tie your horse directly to a ring—there should always be a loop of breakable string that can snap easily in case the horse panics and pulls back.

CREATE A LOOP

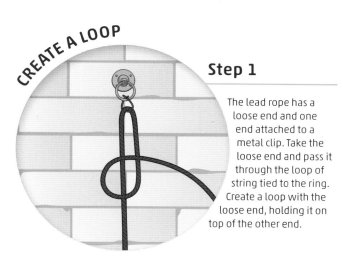

Step 1

The lead rope has a loose end and one end attached to a metal clip. Take the loose end and pass it through the loop of string tied to the ring. Create a loop with the loose end, holding it on top of the other end.

MAKE A SECOND LOOP

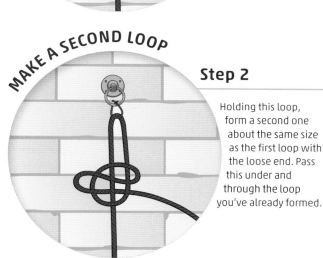

Step 2

Holding this loop, form a second one about the same size as the first loop with the loose end. Pass this under and through the loop you've already formed.

PULL IT TIGHT

Step 3

Leaving this second loop loose, pull on the knot and the rope that is attached to the horse. The knot will untie quickly when you pull on the loose end, but it will stay secure for the horse.

GET BRAIDING

FROM THE TOP

Step 1

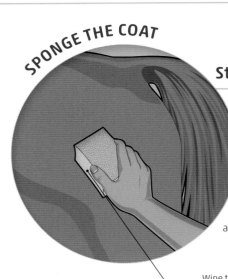

Brush your horse's tail and dampen the section you're going to braid. Take a small section of hair from the center and from each side of the tail at the top, and cross them one over the other to start the braid.

A well-brushed tail is much easier to separate into strands.

KEEP IT EVEN

Step 2

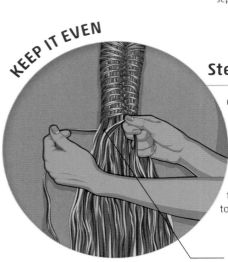

Carry on working down the tail, bringing in new sections of hair from the back at regular intervals and from alternate sides and joining them into the braid. Braid almost to the end of the dock.

Small sections should be taken from the back of the tail.

A TIDY FINISH

Step 3

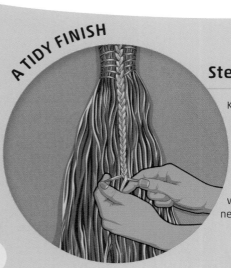

Keep braiding to the end of the tail but stop adding new sections of hair. Double the long braid back on itself and secure it in place with hair bands or a needle and thread.

PATTERN TIME

SPONGE THE COAT

Step 1

Creating temporary marks on a horse's hindquarters is easy to do. Start by using a wet sponge to dampen the area you want to pattern. Then spray the hair with a conditioning spray.

Wipe the sponge in the same direction as the hair.

DRAW THE SQUARES

Step 2

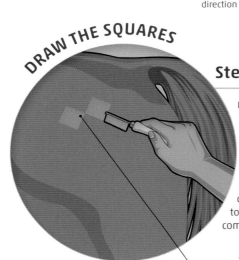

Using a quarter marking comb, create the first square by gently brushing downward. Leave a gap uncombed, then move the brush downward again to create the next combed square.

The combed squares appear a different color shade than the uncombed squares.

IT'S A CHESSBOARD!

Step 3

Build up the chessboard pattern, alternating combed and uncombed squares. Fewer squares tend to look better than too many, so don't cover too much of the horse's hindquarters with the pattern.

Show time!

As your riding improves, you might like to show off your skills at an event and try to win a cup or rosette. To improve your chance of winning, you'll first need to get your horse looking its best. There are lots of ways to do this, from braiding your horse's mane and tail to creating a pattern on its coat.

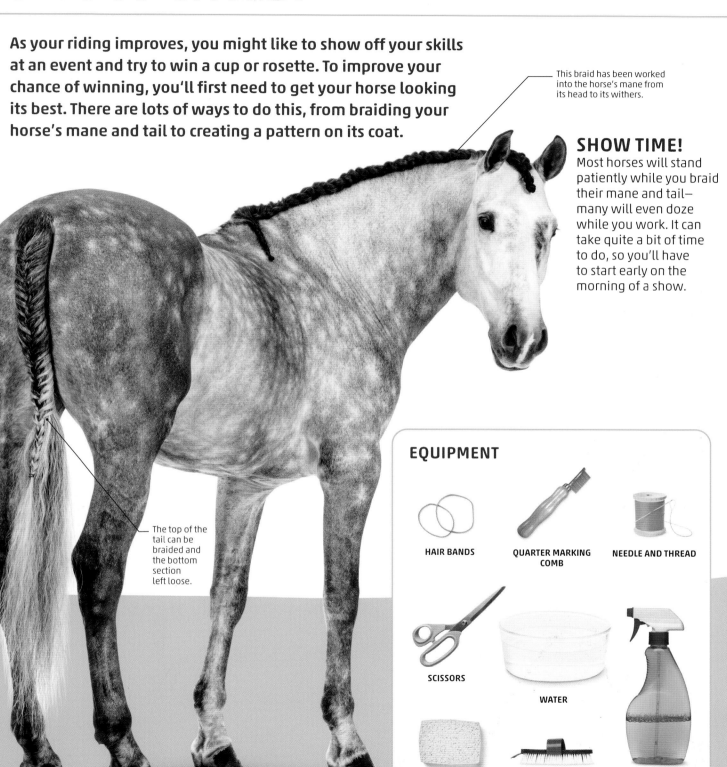

This braid has been worked into the horse's mane from its head to its withers.

The top of the tail can be braided and the bottom section left loose.

SHOW TIME!

Most horses will stand patiently while you braid their mane and tail—many will even doze while you work. It can take quite a bit of time to do, so you'll have to start early on the morning of a show.

EQUIPMENT

HAIR BANDS

QUARTER MARKING COMB

NEEDLE AND THREAD

SCISSORS

WATER

SPONGE

BODY BRUSH

CONDITIONING SPRAY

Horse skills

What to wear

When riding, it's important that the clothes you wear are safe and comfortable. You need stretchy trousers that won't rub your legs, and boots with a slight heel. You must also wear a riding hat to protect yourself— riding schools usually have hats to lend out.

Jodhpurs are specially made for riding, with extra padding around the knees.

HARD HAT
A hard hat is essential for safe riding, especially when you're learning, but it needs to be fitted correctly. Many hats have a three-point safety harness that buckles under your chin.

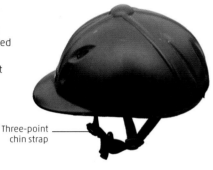

Three-point chin strap

BOOTS
You can choose to wear long or short boots. Regardless of your choice, it is important that your footwear has a slight heel, which stops your foot from sliding through the stirrup irons.

Boots shouldn't have laces or buckles, as these could get caught in the stirrups.

BODY PROTECTOR
A foam-filled body protector fits over your clothes and protects your body in case you have a fall. It is important to wear one if you begin learning to jump.

A body protector should have a safety standard label.

CASUAL WEAR
If you ride often, you soon realize that comfortable clothes are essential. If it's cold, a windproof or waterproof jacket helps to keep you warm, and gloves help you to grip the reins. Long boots protect your jodhpurs from getting dirty.

A rosette shows that you and your horse have placed in a competition.

FORMAL WEAR

If you enter competitions, you may have to dress up in a shirt and tie, jacket, clean jodhpurs, and shiny boots. This is particularly the case for dressage. Top-level dressage competitors must wear cotton gloves, too.

If you wear a coat or jacket, always make sure it is buttoned up so it doesn't flap and scare your horse.

A competition judge will verify that your horse is wearing clean tack.

Early lessons

During your first riding lessons, you'll be paired up with a horse that is used to beginners and the right size for you. You'll get to know your horse and work with an instructor to gradually build up your confidence in the saddle.

It's important to maintain a line from the elbow through the reins to the bit.

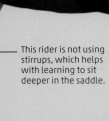

This rider is not using stirrups, which helps with learning to sit deeper in the saddle.

GETTING SETTLED

Step 1

After helping you into the saddle, the instructor will stand to the side of your horse and check that the stirrups have been set at the right length for your legs. Once you and the horse are comfortable, the lesson can begin!

READY TO GO

Step 2

Led by your instructor, the horse will walk to the arena. Give yourself a little while to get used to the feel of a horse moving beneath you —it can seem a bit strange at first!

A lead rope should be held with two hands.

164

ON THE LUNGE

In early lessons, the instructor keeps control of the horse on behalf of the rider, either using a lead rope or lunge rein. Both these methods mean that new riders can focus completely on keeping their balance and learning how to sit correctly. In a lunge lesson, a horse moves in a circle around the riding instructor on the end of a long line. Once a rider has had a few lessons, they can try riding without stirrups, in order to learn how to sit deeper in the saddle.

The riding instructor gives commands to the horse.

A long lungeing whip is used to encourage the horse.

Depending on how confident the rider is, the instructor can vary the length of the lunge rein.

GROUP RIDING LESSON

Group lessons help riders learn to control their horses when there are other horses around too. Group lessons can take place in an arena, or an instructor might take riders farther afield, out on a hack into the local countryside, for example. Most people in a group should be at the same level, so that nobody gets left behind and everyone has fun.

Starting out

MOUNTING

Learning how to get on and off a horse safely, known as mounting and dismounting, is one of the first things you'll be taught when riding. Most people do it from the ground, as shown here, but some people use a large step called a mounting block.

STAND NEXT TO THE PONY

Step 1

Stand next to the pony's left shoulder, facing the tail, and take the reins in your left hand. Lift your left foot and put it into the stirrup. Push your toe downward so that you don't poke the pony in the stomach.

Use your right hand to turn the stirrup iron toward you.

GET READY

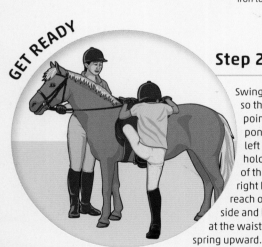

Step 2

Swing your left foot so that the toe points toward the pony's head. Your left hand should hold the pommel of the saddle. Your right hand should reach over to the other side and hold the saddle at the waist. Get ready to spring upward.

SWING THE RIGHT LEG OVER

Step 3

Leap up, lifting your right leg carefully up and over the back of the saddle. Make sure you sit down on the saddle gently.

Try to push your toe down as you mount.

DISMOUNTING

SITTING COMFORTABLY

Once you're seated, make sure both your feet are in the stirrups, with the ball of each foot resting on them. Relax into your seat and listen to the instructor as they will be getting ready to check the girth, the length of the stirrup leathers, and the way you're holding the reins.

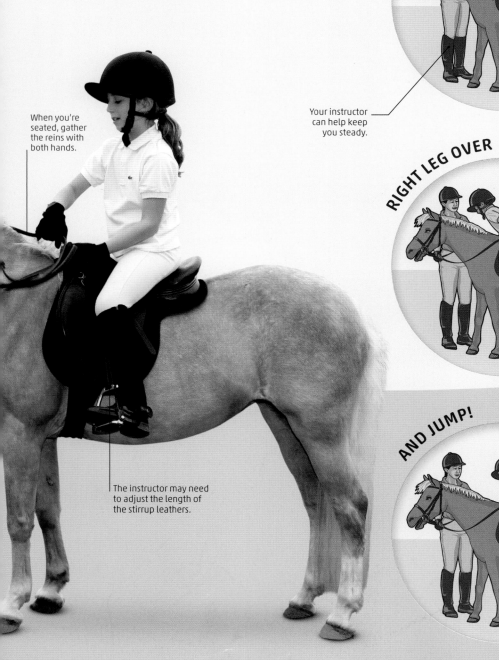

When you're seated, gather the reins with both hands.

The instructor may need to adjust the length of the stirrup leathers.

PREPARE TO DISMOUNT

Your instructor can help keep you steady.

Step 1

There are different ways to dismount, but this method is used in classical, or English, riding. Put the reins into your left hand and take both feet out of the stirrups. Lean slightly forward in the saddle.

RIGHT LEG OVER

Step 2

Lean farther forward and, holding onto the front of the saddle, bring your right leg up and over the pony's back. Lean over the saddle as your body turns and hold the front and center of the saddle.

AND JUMP!

Step 3

You're now ready to jump down. Try to keep your legs away from the pony's legs, so you don't accidentally kick them. Aim to land facing forward, but most importantly, don't let go of the reins!

Getting comfortable

Once you're up on your horse or pony, relax. Horses are sensitive to what is happening around them, and if you feel content, they will too. It's now time to think about how you hold your reins, where your legs should be, and the length of your stirrups.

IN CONTROL

A well-trained horse will stand patiently while your instructor adjusts the girth and stirrups. Once that is done, it's time to begin thinking about natural aids. Natural aids are the way you communicate with your horse, and it's done with your legs, body position, hands, and voice.

The reins shouldn't be too tight, nor should they hang too loosely.

TIGHTENING THE GIRTH

Horses often expand their bellies when the saddle is put on, so it's good to make sure the girth is tight. Nobody wants a saddle to slip under the horse halfway through a lesson! It should be possible to slip the flat of your hand between the horse and the girth, but no more. When you are learning, your riding instructor will adjust the girth, but you'll soon learn how to check it yourself.

FEET AND STIRRUPS

When riding, keep the widest part of your foot, known as the ball of the foot, on the bar of the stirrup. Always try to keep your toes slightly up and your heels down, but not if this causes you to tense your body.

SITTING PROPERLY

Sit up tall, keep your back straight, but stay relaxed. Hold the reins with both hands. Don't grip with your legs— let them rest lightly against the horse's sides. Use the reins to keep a light contact with the horse's mouth, aiming for a line from your elbow, through your hands, to the bit.

Now you're in the saddle, you're ready to start learning to ride. Remember, **stay relaxed**!

HOLDING THE REINS

To hold your reins correctly, curl your hands into loose fists, with the reins threaded in between your little and ring fingers and then out between your thumbs and index fingers. Your thumbs should be on top. Use the reins gently.

Which way?

It's now time to discover how to ask your pony to go where you want it to go. Riding school ponies are trained to understand particular signals that they're given by their rider. Once you learn these signals, controlling your pony becomes easier.

MAKING A RIGHT TURN

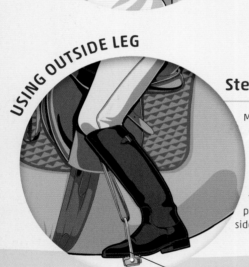

Step 1

To turn right, begin by feeling the right rein by slightly rolling your hand over to the right to ease the rein back. Don't pull—your pony can sense small movements. As you feel your pony turn its head, move your left hand forward.

USING OUTSIDE LEG

Step 2

Move your outside leg (in this case, the left leg) behind the girth. To keep your pony from swinging out its hindquarters as it turns right, put slight pressure on the pony's side here with your leg.

Keep the ball of your foot on the stirrup.

USING INSIDE LEG

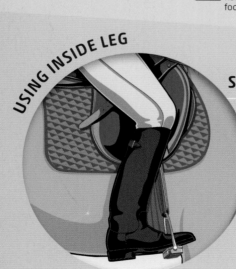

Step 3

Press inward with your inside leg (in this case, the right leg) to encourage your pony to move forward. It might help to imagine that you're turning your pony around this leg.

WHERE TO LOOK

It's important always to be aware of what you and your pony are doing. When moving straight, keep your gaze between your pony's ears. If you want to change direction, it helps to turn your body in the direction you want to go.

This rider is exaggerating the hand movement to show how you open the rein when turning rather than pulling it back.

Try not to flap your legs around as it will confuse your pony.

IMPROVING YOUR STEERING

A short obstacle course of cones is a good way to practise your steering after you've learnt the basics. Remember to look where you're heading as you weave through them, adjusting your hands and legs as needed.

NECK REINING

Some horses respond to the feel of the rein against their necks—a method called neck reining. To steer, this rider moves their hands to the side they want to turn toward.

STOP!

To practice stopping, use two parallel poles placed a little bit apart. As your horse moves between the poles, sit back and squeeze the reins by turning your wrists in a little. You may need to pull your arms back slightly, but never yank on the reins.

Trot on!

As you start to feel more confident, it might be time to try out going a bit faster. If you feel eager, you're ready to learn to trot! There are two types of trot: sitting trot and rising trot. With its 1-2 pace, trotting can feel bumpy at first, but it gets easier as you relax into the rhythm.

Always try to look ahead.

Keep your back straight, but relax your lower back into the saddle.

SITTING TROT

You may find it challenging at first, but the only way to improve your sitting trot is to keep practicing. You'll feel the muscles on the horse's back moving as it's trotting. Adjust the muscles in your lower back, belly, and hips to stay connected with your horse. Try not to grip tightly with your legs as it will make you bounce and this will affect the horse's movement and posture.

RISING TROT

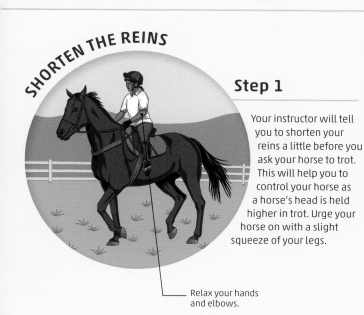

SHORTEN THE REINS

Step 1

Your instructor will tell you to shorten your reins a little before you ask your horse to trot. This will help you to control your horse as a horse's head is held higher in trot. Urge your horse on with a slight squeeze of your legs.

— Relax your hands and elbows.

KEEP YOUR HANDS STILL

Step 2

As your horse moves into trot, stay seated until you pick up the rhythm of the trot. Then begin to gently rise and sit, aiming to match the movement of your horse's front legs. Keep your hands fairly still throughout.

— Try not to flap your legs against the horse's sides.

CHANGE THE DIAGONAL

When a horse trots, its legs move together in diagonal pairs (shown in yellow and blue). The switch from one pair to the other is known as changing the diagonal. To do this, you simply need to sit for one extra beat, then begin rising again. It's important that you keep to the rhythm of your horse and do not sit too heavily.

FIRST BEAT
On the first beat, rise as normal. Here, the left foreleg and the right hind leg of the horse is in a diagonal pair (shown in blue).

SECOND BEAT
Sit on the second beat as the horse moves with the right foreleg and the left hind leg in diagonal pairs (shown in yellow).

FIRST BEAT
To switch pairs, remain seated on the first beat instead of returning to rise as normal. Rise on the next beat and continue as before.

LEADING LEG

A canter has a three-beat rhythm, with a leading leg. A hind hoof hits the ground (first beat), followed by the other hind hoof and its opposite front hoof (second beat), then the other front hoof (third beat). This foreleg is the leading leg. If moving clockwise around an arena, the leading leg should be the front right leg.

The horse moves its head up and down quite a bit at canter.

Keep the upper body as still as possible.

READY TO CANTER

Moving from one gait to another, such as from trot to canter, is called a transition. When learning to canter, your instructor will suggest transitioning from trot to canter as you approach a corner of the arena. This is because it's easier to move into canter on the correct leading leg as the horse approaches a corner.

Keep your legs relaxed—try not to grip with your lower leg in canter.

This horse is leading with its right leg, which is the last leg to hit the ground.

Learning to canter

As soon as you're comfortable in trot, it's time to ease yourself into the next gait, and learn to canter. Cantering is often described as a rocking horse motion, and it is easier to learn than the trot. It's also usually faster, though a controlled canter can actually be rather slow. You'll start learning to canter by moving into it from a trot.

LEARNING TO GALLOP

After cantering, the next thing to learn is the gallop. For a gallop, the rider needs to bend forward from the hips and shift their weight just out of the saddle. Because of this position, it's easiest to shorten the stirrups slightly before a gallop. A horse can't gallop for long as it takes a lot of energy.

START IN TROT

Step 1

If you feel balanced in a rising trot, stop rising and sit in the saddle. Sit up and look ahead to where you're going.

SIT UPRIGHT

Step 2

Sit upright for a few strides and squeeze with your inside leg on the girth, and your outside leg behind the girth, to get the horse to canter. Do not tip forward. Feel the horse's movement through your lower back. Keep your upper body still.

GENTLY SQUEEZE

Step 3

Feel the beat of the canter in your hips and move with it. Keep your legs where they are, squeezing if necessary to keep your horse in its canter.

BACK TO TROT

Step 4

When you're ready to go back into trot, stop moving your hips, sit up, and close your fingers around the reins. Don't ever yank back on the reins.

Getting to know the arena

Many people learn to ride in a fenced area known as a riding arena or manège. It's a safe place to learn, where the riding instructor can stand in the center and call instructions. When you first start out in an arena, you'll usually follow a "lead" horse and rider (known as a "leading file"), but as you develop your skills, you'll start to ride independently.

The markers provide guides for different exercises. To ride in a circle, for example, you might start at A, go round to X, and then back to A.

K

THE STANDARD ARENA

The arena has letters, called markers, at certain positions around it, laid out in a particular order. These markers are used when teaching. There are also three points in the center, D, X, and G, which aren't usually marked.

There needs to be a distance the length of a horse between each rider.

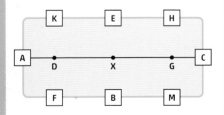

K	E	H
A — D — X — G — C
F	B	M

FROM K TO M

There are various exercises that involve riding across the arena from one marker to another.

CHANGING THE REIN

These horses are crossing the arena diagonally to "change the rein." It's a phrase that's often heard in the arena. It means to move across the arena to change direction—for example, from clockwise to counterclockwise. These horses are in the process of crossing the arena diagonally by traveling from K to M on the other side.

PASSING LEFT TO LEFT

When a rider meets another rider coming in the opposite direction, they should pass left side to left side. There should always be at least a pony's width between two passing riders to avoid any collisions.

ARENA EXERCISES

The arena is a safe place in which to try out new exercises and build up confidence. Some exercises involve the rider moving while the horse remains still.

REACH FORWARD

To improve your balance, your riding instructor may ask you to lean forward and touch your pony's ears, or reach backward to touch its tail.

REACHING UP AND DOWN

This exercise involves stretching up with one hand, then down to touch your toes. Try to touch each hand to the opposite toe.

E

The markers are usually on stiff boards so it doesn't matter if they get wet.

This pair is the lead horse and rider—the others follow behind them.

Ready to jump!

If you've learned to trot and canter, you'll probably feel ready for the ultimate horse-riding thrill—learning to jump! When a horse jumps, it leaps up and forward, then stretches its neck out before landing and returning to a canter.

JUMPING POSITION

Having a good jumping position is all about knowing how to react to a horse's movements. As the rider, you have to change your body position at the right time to help the horse keep its balance.

The rider must keep their gaze ahead.

Keeping a straight back, the rider folds down over the horse's shoulders as it rises into the jump.

The hands move slightly forward as the horse stretches out its neck.

The rider lifts up out of the saddle.

Shortening the stirrups will help the rider to keep their balance when the horse jumps.

Jumping a spread fence like this one takes a lot of practice.

This horse is wearing overreach boots, which protect the front feet if the back feet hit them on landing.

THE APPROACH

Step 1

As you approach the jump, keep your eyes ahead and let the horse find its own stride. Steer your horse toward the center of the jump.

LEARNING TO JUMP

Your riding instructor will increase the height you jump in stages, beginning with trotting poles and moving on to cross poles. From there you'll soon be tackling an upright jump with poles that can be raised as you grow in confidence.

TROTTING POLES
These evenly spaced, striped poles let you practice your jumping position and get used to the horse's strides changing as it moves over obstacles.

CROSS POLES
Cross poles are the easiest type of jump. The horse will tend to head automatically for the center where the jump is lowest. As you improve, the height of the poles can be raised.

TAKING OFF

Step 2

Keeping your back as straight as possible and looking forward, fold your body down over the horse's neck. Your body weight should sink down into your heels.

THE LANDING

Step 4

As the horse lands, unfold your body to sit more upright. Think of your knees and ankles as springs that absorb the impact of the landing.

IN FLIGHT

Step 3

As the horse's body levels out, keep your position but get ready to sit back in the saddle as soon as you feel the horse's front dropping to land.

THE GETAWAY

Step 5

A horse will head away from a jump in canter. Adjust your hands to keep a soft contact with the horse's mouth. Make sure you keep a good canter and look ahead to the next jump.

Mounted games

Played all around the world, horseback games and competitions are fast-paced and thrilling. These events test riders and their horses on a variety of skills, including endurance, speed, and bravery, as well as their ability to work together. Some games are solo, while others are played in teams.

The rider uses one arm to hold the lance and the other arm to control the horse.

TENT PEGGING

Individuals or teams of riders compete against each other in the sport of tent pegging. The aim is to head toward a small wooden peg that lies on the ground—at a gallop—and pick it up by spearing it with a lance or sword. Tent pegging has been played in India since at least the 4th century BCE, and it is still popular all over the world.

The lance has a sharp point at one end.

The peg is speared, then raised off the ground.

180

PATO

The game of Pato is Argentina's national sport. Two teams of four players battle to grab a six-handled ball and throw it through a vertical ring on top of a pole to score goals. Variations of Pato are played around the world, but elsewhere it is known as horseball.

GYMKHANA

Lots of children enjoy gymkhanas, which are full of different races on and off horseback. For stepping stones, shown here, riders dismount and step across a number of upturned buckets. They then leap back into the saddle and race with their ponies to the finish.

BARREL RACING

At a rodeo, riders enjoy a number of games that showcase Western riding. In barrel racing, a horse and rider dash around an arena against the clock, making sharp turns around three barrels arranged in a triangular pattern. Riders who knock over a barrel get a time penalty of five seconds or more.

HORSEBACK ARCHERY

Believe it or not, it's possible for a rider to fire an arrow and hit a small target from the back of a moving horse. Japanese Yabusame archers shoot blunt-headed arrows at three wooden targets, one by one, all while their horses gallop along a course.

Rodeo events **showcase the thrilling** side of herding cattle.

A rodeo is all about riders lassoing cattle, barrel racing, and taking part in frantic relays in which batons are passed between galloping riders. Rodeo competitions were originally set up by cowboys wanting to show off their herding skills. Nowadays, everyone can take part – including children!

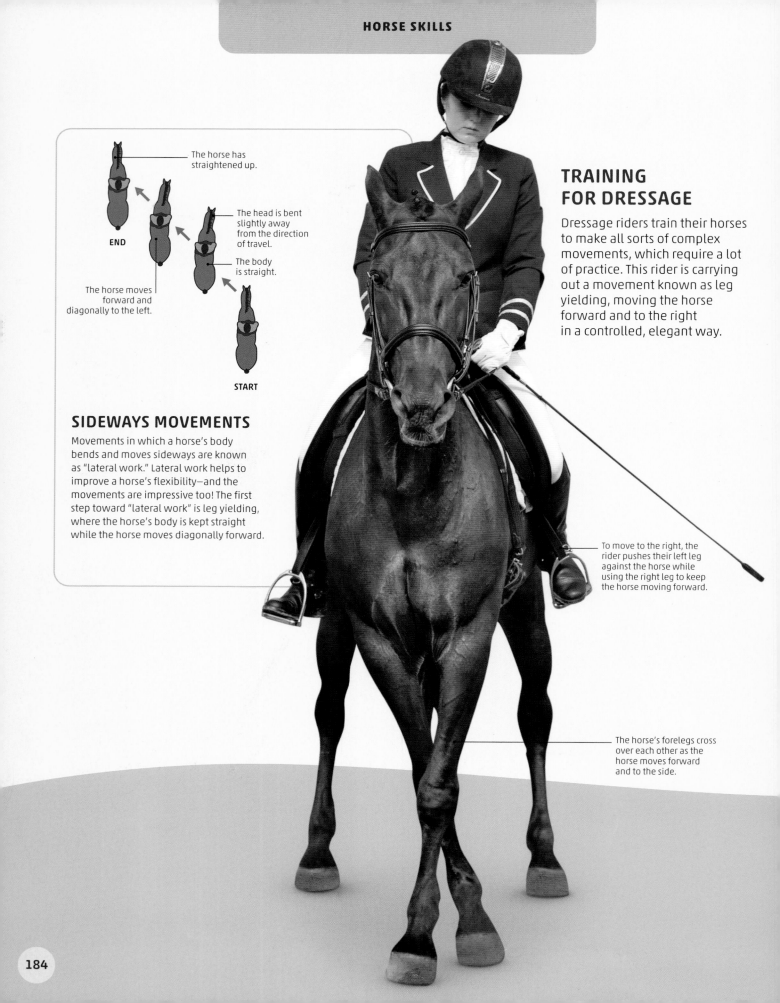

The horse has straightened up.

END

The head is bent slightly away from the direction of travel.

The body is straight.

The horse moves forward and diagonally to the left.

START

TRAINING FOR DRESSAGE

Dressage riders train their horses to make all sorts of complex movements, which require a lot of practice. This rider is carrying out a movement known as leg yielding, moving the horse forward and to the right in a controlled, elegant way.

SIDEWAYS MOVEMENTS

Movements in which a horse's body bends and moves sideways are known as "lateral work." Lateral work helps to improve a horse's flexibility—and the movements are impressive too! The first step toward "lateral work" is leg yielding, where the horse's body is kept straight while the horse moves diagonally forward.

To move to the right, the rider pushes their left leg against the horse while using the right leg to keep the horse moving forward.

The horse's forelegs cross over each other as the horse moves forward and to the side.

Advanced skills

In riding, there are always more skills you can learn to help you become a better rider. And it's not just riders who can learn new skills—horses are also taught advanced movements, such as turn on the forehand, rein back, and sideways movements.

OPENING A GATE

It's tricky to position your horse, stay in control, and open (or shut) a gate all at the same time—but it is possible. Learning new skills will help you if you encounter obstacles such as gates while out on rides.

TURN ON THE FOREHAND

During a turn on the forehand, the horse moves in a semicircle, keeping its front legs in the same place—it doesn't move forward or backward. To move, the horse crosses and uncrosses its hind legs in one direction, while hardly moving its front legs.

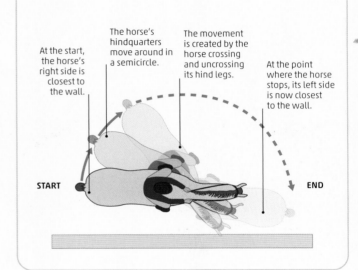

At the start, the horse's right side is closest to the wall.

The horse's hindquarters move around in a semicircle.

The movement is created by the horse crossing and uncrossing its hind legs.

At the point where the horse stops, its left side is now closest to the wall.

START

END

REIN BACK

Rein back is a two-beat movement in which a horse moves backwards. It's very useful for when you need to move your horse around in tight spaces, or if you're opening or shutting a gate. Rein back always begins and ends in halt.

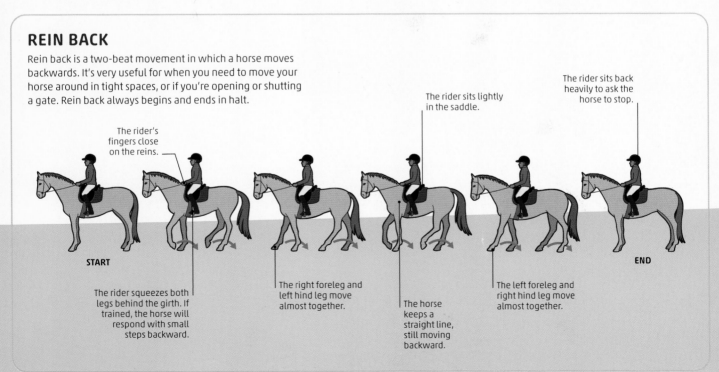

The rider's fingers close on the reins.

The rider sits lightly in the saddle.

The rider sits back heavily to ask the horse to stop.

START

END

The rider squeezes both legs behind the girth. If trained, the horse will respond with small steps backward.

The right foreleg and left hind leg move almost together.

The horse keeps a straight line, still moving backward.

The left foreleg and right hind leg move almost together.

It takes about **five years to train a horse** to compete at top-level dressage events.

Grand Prix dressage—shown here by Japanese competitor Akane Kuroki riding Toots—is performed at the Olympic Games. It takes a lot of strength for a horse to perform the movements required, and they need to be clever to remember them, too.

GLOSSARY

Terms in bold are defined elsewhere in the glossary.

AIDS
The methods used by a rider to "talk" to their horse using their body position, legs, hands, and voice.

ARENA
An enclosed area in which riders have riding lessons. It's also called a manège.

BIT
The part of the **bridle** that is held in a horse's mouth.

BLACKSMITH
A person who is trained to look after a horse's hooves.

BRAND
An identification mark that is made on the skin of a horse to identify its owner.

BRIDLE
The harness attached to the horse's head, used by riders to help control their horses with the **reins**.

CANNON BONE
The lower foreleg of a horse, between the knee and the **fetlock**.

CANTER
A three-beat **gait** in which two diagonal feet hit the ground at the same time and the other two feet hit the ground separately.

CANTLE
The raised section at the back of a **saddle**.

CONFORMATION
The shape of a horse.

CRIB BITING
When a horse bites down on a fence rail, stall door, or post and draws in air.

CROUP
The top of a horse's hindquarters.

DOCK
The muscles and skin covering the vertebrae (spinal bones) in the tail, found at the point where the tail joins the horse's rump.

DRAFT HORSE
See **Heavy horse**.

DRESSAGE
A sport that involves a trained horse acting on the signals of its skilled rider to perform specialized movements.

EVENTING
An event where riders compete across three disciplines: **dressage**, cross-country, and **show jumping**.

FEATHERS
The long hairs found on the lower part of the legs in some breeds of horses.

FERAL
A horse that is related to horses that were once domesticated (used by people) but now lives in the wild.

FETLOCK
The joint at the bottom of a horse's leg, between the **cannon bone** and the **pastern**.

FETUS
The name for a mammal before it is born.

FLEHMEN
A response given by a horse, usually by a **stallion** to a **mare**, when it lifts its top lip to "smell" the air.

FOAL
A young member of the horse family that is less than a year old.

FORELOCK
The hair that grows from the horse's **poll**, and hangs down over its forehead.

FROG
The soft inner part of a horse's hoof that is shaped like a triangle.

GAIT
A term describing a horse's movements. Most horses have four gaits: **walk**, **trot**, **canter**, and **gallop**. Some horses have additional, specialized gaits.

GALLOP
A four-beat **gait**, which is also the fastest.

GIRTH
The strap that holds a **saddle** on a horse.

GROOM
The action of brushing a horse to clean its coat and picking mud and stones out of its hooves.

GYMKHANA
An event with games and competitions carried out on horseback between young riders as individuals or in teams.

HACK
A ride into the countryside.

HALTER
A piece of **tack** that fits around the horse's head. It's used for moving a horse to and from the field, as well as tying up a horse.

HANDS
A unit of measurement, based on the width of a human hand, used to calculate a horse's height. One hand is 4 in (10 cm). Horses are measured from the ground to the top of the **withers**.

HEAVY HORSE
A large, heavily muscled horse that is used for hauling big loads.

LIGHT HORSE
A horse that is used for riding or for pulling carriages. They are smaller than heavy horses but larger than ponies.

LUNGE REIN
A long rein that gives control of a horse in an arena to an instructor, who stands in the center.

MANE
The long hair that grows from the crest (the back of a horse's neck).

MARE
An adult female horse.

NEAR FORE
A horse's front left leg.

NEAR HIND
A horse's rear left leg.

NEAR SIDE
A horse's left side.

OFF FORE
A horse's front right leg.

OFF HIND
A horse's rear right leg.

OFF SIDE
A horse's right side.

PACE
A fast-moving **gait** that is only achieved by a small number of breeds. It is similar to a fast **trot**.

PASTERN
The area between a horse's hoof and its **fetlock** joint.

POINTS
The different parts of a horse, such as its **withers** and **quarters**.

POLL
The area at the top of a horse's head, between and just behind the ears.

POMMEL
The raised part at the front of a **saddle**.

PONY
A type of horse that is fewer than or equal to 14.2 **hands** in height.

QUARTERS
The hind part of a horse, above the hind legs.

REINS
The long straps that run from the **bit** and are held by the rider.

RODEO
A fast-paced event in which riders show their cattle-herding skills.

RUNNING WALK
A special **gait** that only a few horses can do. It is a fast-paced **gait**, in which the horse takes longer steps than when in **walk**.

SADDLE
The seat, usually made from leather, fastened onto the back of a horse for riding.

SHOW JUMPING
A sport in which horses are ridden around a course in an arena that contains a number of fences to jump over. The contestants are given penalty points, called faults, for any errors.

STALLION
A male horse that is more than four years old and hasn't been neutered. A stallion used for breeding is known as a stud.

STEEPLECHASE
A distance horse race over fences and open ditches. Traditionally, a steeplechase was a cross-country race from one village to another.

STIRRUP
A light frame, usually made from metal, that holds the foot of a rider and is attached to the **saddle** by a stirrup leather.

TACK
The equipment a horse wears, such as the **saddle** and **bridle**, which is used for riding and training the horse.

TÖLT
A four-beat, fast-paced **walk** uniquely associated with Icelandic horses.

TROT
A two-beat **gait** in which the horse's legs move in diagonal pairs, near fore with off fore and off fore with near hind.

WALK
A slow, four-beat **gait** in which each of the horse's legs hits the ground separately.

WESTERN RIDING
A style of riding in which the horse is trained to respond to pressure from the **reins** on its neck and the rider's position in the **saddle**. The **reins** are held in one hand.

WHISKERS
The longer hair that grows near the mouth of many mammals. They are highly sensitive and allow mammals to gather information about their surroundings.

WITHERS
The top of a horse's shoulders.

INDEX

ACKNOWLEDGMENTS

The publisher would like to thank the following for their kind assistance in the preparation of this book:

Helen Peters for indexing; Victoria Pyke for proofreading. Senior Jacket Designer Suhita Dharamjit; Senior DTP Designers Harish Aggarwal and Jagtar Singh; Jackets Editorial Coordinator Priyanka Sharma; and Production Manager Pankaj Sharma.

The publisher would like to thank the following for their kind permission to reproduce their photographs:

(Key: a-above; b-below/bottom; c-center; tc-top center; bc-below/bottom center; cl-center left; cr-center right; cla-center left above; clb-center left below/bottom; cra-center right above; crb-center right below/bottom; l-left; r-right; t-top, bl-below/bottom left; br-below/bottom right).

1 Courtesy of Ebony Riding Club. 4 Dorling Kindersley: Stephen Oliver / Appaloosa - Golden Nugget Sally Chaplin (b). 10 Alamy Stock Photo: Classic Image (bl); North Wind Picture Archives (clb). Bridgeman Images: (crb); Peter Newark American Pictures (br). Dorling Kindersley: Kit Houghton / Chateau de Saumur - Musee de Cheval (cra). Museum and Galleries of Ljubljana: Andrej Peunik (tr). Photo Scala, Florence: bpk, Bildagentur fuer Kunst, Kultur und (cla). 11 Alamy Stock Photo: Adam Eastland (cr). Getty Images: Romilly Lockyer (br); Bob Thomas / Popperfoto (bl). Shutterstock.com: The Art Archive (t). SuperStock: DeAgostini (cl). 12-13 Getty Images: Gonzalo Azumendi. 14 Dorling Kindersley: Blackpool Zoo, Lancashire, UK (bl); Dreamstime.com: Bahadir Yeniceri / Suzbah (tl); Dreamstime.com: Gorshkov13 (tr). 14-15 Dorling Kindersley: Jerry Young (bc). 15 Dorling Kindersley: Dreamstime.com: Smellme (bc); Dreamstime.com: Eric Isselee (br). 16-17 Alamy Stock Photo: imageBROKER (bc). 16 Alamy Stock Photo: Leo de Groot (t). Shutterstock.com: Danita Delimont (c). 17 Alamy Stock

Photo: Juniors Bildarchiv GmbH (br); Nature Picture Library (t, c). 18-19 Getty Images: tom_kolossa. 22-23 Dorling Kindersley: Dreamstime.com: Kseniya Abramova / Tristana. 24 Alamy Stock Photo: agefotostock (cl). 26-27 Alamy Stock Photo: Gareth McCormack. 28 Alamy Stock Photo: infinity (cl). 28-29 Getty Images: Abramova_Kseniya (b). 29 Alamy Stock Photo: Ivan Kmit (br). Depositphotos Inc: castenoid (tl); picsbyst (cr). 30 Alamy Stock Photo: RooM the Agency (b) Dorling Kindersley: Dreamstime.com: Isselee (t). 31 Alamy Stock Photo: John Warburton-Lee Photography (cr). 32 Alamy Stock Photo: Juniors Bildarchiv GmbH (tl); Nature Picture Library (b). Getty Images: Ellende (tc). Shutterstock.com: anakondasp (tr). 33 Alamy Stock Photo: Elisa Bistocchi (br). naturepl.com: Carol Walker (tc). Shutterstock.com: C. Hamilton (tr); kyslynskahal (tl). 34-35 Alamy Stock Photo: Nature Picture Library. 36 Alamy Stock Photo: Juniors Bildarchiv GmbH (cr). Dorling Kindersley: Bob Langrish / Cleveland Bay - Oaten Mainbrace Courtesy of Mr and Mrs Dimmock (tl). Dreamstime.com: Peterll (crb). 37 Alamy Stock Photo: Life on white (clb); Life on white (br). Dreamstime.com: Isselee (crb). 38 Alamy Stock Photo: Mark J. Barrett (bl); Tierfotoagentur (c, bc); Chris Strickland (br). 42 123RF.com: Isselee Eric Philippe (bl). 43 Alamy Stock Photo: Agencja Fotograficzna Caro (t). 46 Dreamstime.com: Alexia Khruscheva. 47 Dreamstime.com: Tamara Didenko. 50-51 Dreamstime.com: Dziurek. 54-55 Alamy Stock Photo: agefotostock. 60-61 Bob Langrish. 64 Alamy Stock Photo: Panther Media GmbH. 66-67 Spanish Riding School: Rene Van Bakel. 74 Dorling Kindersley: Stephen Oliver / Appaloosa - Golden Nugget Sally Chaplin. 76-77 Everett Marc Photographer. 82-83 bnps.co.uk: Phil Yeomans. 86-87 Shutterstock.com: Lois GoBe. 92-93 Shutterstock.com: Goyo Romero. 96-97 Alamy Stock Photo: Nature Picture Library. 102-103 Getty Images: David Clapp. 108-109 Getty Images: Feifei Cui-Paoluzzo. 116-117 Batzaya Choijiljav. 120-121 Getty Images: Ulet Ifansasti. 125 Dorling Kindersley: Pegasus, Kilverstone Wildlife Park.

129 123RF.com: pumbitaurelio (cr). Alamy Stock Photo: Ethel Poindexter / Stockimo (c). 130-131 Getty Images: Nicolas McComber. 133 Alamy Stock Photo: Kyryl Gorlov (tl); WireStock (cl); Reinhard Tiburzy (c). Dreamstime.com: Casey Martin (tr). Getty Images: Tim Platt (cr). Science Photo Library: Caia Image (tc). 134 Dreamstime.com: Atman (tr); Petr Malyshev (cla). 136 123RF.com: nattawut lakjit (c). 140 Alamy Stock Photo: Nicole Ciscato. 141 Alamy Stock Photo: Agencja Fotograficzna Caro (tr); Imagebroker (cl). Shutterstock.com: Peter Titmuss (tl). 144 Alamy Stock Photo: Agencja Fotograficzna Caro (b). Shutterstock.com: oscar0 (t). 145 Shutterstock.com: horsemen (tl). 146 Alamy Stock Photo: fotografz (b). 148 Alamy Stock Photo: Natalie Anakonda (cra); Imagebroker (tl); Split Seconds (tr); F1online digitale Bildagentur GmbH (cla); Christian Hartmann (clb); Cindy Hopkins (crb) Dorling Kindersley: Geoff Brightling / Walsall Leather Museum (br). Zilco Europe Ltd: (bl). 149 123RF.com: Irina Palei (cl). Alamy Stock Photo: Natalie Anakonda (bl); Michele and Tom Grimm (cla); H. Mark Weidman Photography (cra); David Morgan (clb); Theo Fitzhugh (crb); Dorling Kindersley ltd (br). Getty Images: Westhoff (cr). 150-151 Getty Images: Liu Jin. 153 Getty Images: acceptfoto. 156 Courtesy of Ebony Riding Club: (t). 157 Courtesy of Jasmine Harding-Heitzmann: (cl). Kit Houghton / Houghton's Horses: (bl). 159 Alamy Stock Photo: LAMB (cr/ needle & thread); Life on white. Top Notch Equestrian: (cr/Quarter marking comb). 162 Dorling Kindersley: iStock: Weenee (cr). Courtesy of Jasmine Harding-Heitzmann. 163 Courtesy of Ebony Riding Club. 165 Alamy Stock Photo: Steve Hawkins Photography (br). 168-169 Courtesy of Ebony Riding Club. 169 Alamy Stock Photo: Imagebroker (r). 172 Shutterstock.com: Skumer. 174 Bob Langrish: Courtesy Urbana Riding Club, (rider: Kristin Johnson). 175 Getty Images: Adie Bush (cl). 176 Bob Langrish: Courtesy of Urbana Riding Club, (rider: Kayleigh McDonald). 177 Alamy Stock Photo: Dorling Kindersley ltd (tr). Bob Langrish: Courtesy of Urbana Riding Club, (rider: Natalie Hayes) (b). 178 Bob Langrish: Courtesy of Urbana Riding Club, (rider: Kayleigh McDonald). 179 Alamy Stock Photo:

GV Images (cra). Getty Images: acceptfoto (tr). 180 Getty Images: Tariq Sulemani. 181 Alamy Stock Photo: Sport In Pictures (tr); ZUMA Press, Inc. (bl). Dreamstime.com: Jordi Salas (tl). Getty Images: Glenn Waters (br). 182-183 Getty Images: Scott Olson. 184 Alamy Stock Photo: Elena Vagengeym. 185 Alamy Stock Photo: Turnip Towers (cl). 186-187 Getty Images: Sean M. Haffey.

Cover images:
Front: Shutterstock.com: Olga_i; Back: Alamy Stock Photo: Tierfotoagentur (cr); Getty Images: Nicolas McComber (cl).

All other images :
© Dorling Kindersley

For further information see: www.dkimages.com